Dying to See You!

Dying to See You!

Light Tetramorphic Essays on
Life, Love, and Death

Charles Taliaferro

FOREWORD BY
Catherine Wilcox

CASCADE Books • Eugene, Oregon

DYING TO SEE YOU!
Light Tetramorphic Essays on Life, Love, and Death

Copyright © 2025 Charles Taliaferro. All rights reserved. Except for brief quotations in critical publications or reviews, no part of this book may be reproduced in any manner without prior written permission from the publisher. Write: Permissions, Wipf and Stock Publishers, 199 W. 8th Ave., Suite 3, Eugene, OR 97401.

Cascade Books
An Imprint of Wipf and Stock Publishers
199 W. 8th Ave., Suite 3
Eugene, OR 97401

www.wipfandstock.com

PAPERBACK ISBN: 979-8-3852-3273-4
HARDCOVER ISBN: 979-8-3852-3274-1
EBOOK ISBN: 979-8-3852-3275-8

Cataloguing-in-Publication data:

Names: Taliaferro, Charles [author]. | Wilcox, Catherine [foreword].
Title: Dying to see you! : light tetramorphic essays on life, love, and death / by Charles Taliaferro ; foreword by Catherine Wilcox.
Description: Eugene, OR: Cascade Books, 2025
Identifiers: ISBN 979-8-3852-3273-4 (paperback) | ISBN 979-8-3852-3274-1 (hardcover) | ISBN 979-8-3852-3275-8 (ebook)
Subjects: LCSH: Essays. | Life—Religious aspects—Christianity. | Love—Religious aspects—Christianity. | Death—Religious aspects—Christianity. | Essayists.
Classification: BV4900 T35 2025 (paperback) | BV4900 (ebook)

VERSION NUMBER 05/19/25

This book is dedicated with love and deep gratitude to two mentors: Petrus Meyeringh, a luminous guide akin to Gandalf, who rescued me from perilous wandering in my youth; and to Margaret Miles, who has been exemplary in employing rigorous scholarship and art history to contribute to contemporary Christian spirituality.

And to Dr. Sally Engebretson and Dr. Todd Shea, repairers of the world, *par excellence*. Without them, this book would not have been written.

The Clod and the Pebble

"Love seeketh not itself to please,
Nor for itself hath any care,
But for another gives its ease,
And builds a Heaven in Hell's despair."

So sung a little Clod of Clay
Trodden with the cattle's feet,
But a Pebble of the brook
Warbled out these metres meet:

"Love seeketh only self to please,
To bind another to its delight,
Joys in another's loss of ease,
And builds a Hell in Heaven's despite."

—William Blake[1]

---

1. "The Clod and the Pebble," by William Blake, is included in any complete collection of his poems and at https://www.poetryfoundation.org/poems/43655/the-clod-and-the-pebble.

For an overview of his spirituality, I recommend Jennifer Jesse, *William Blake's Religious Vision: There's a Methodism in His Madness* (New York: Lexington, 2013).

Contents

Foreword by Catherine Wilcox | ix
Acknowledgments | xiii
An Essential Introduction | xv

Part One: **The Winged Human**

1. Dying to See You! | 3
2. Repairing the World | 7
3. Homeward Bound | 12
4. In the Beginning | 15
5. Parables and Parabolic Performances | 18
6. Ransom | 23
7. Prayer Times | 28
8. Somersaults on the Grass | 34

Part Two: **The Ox**

9. The Ox and the Ass | 41
10. Lost and Found | 45
11. Speaking Historically | 48
12. Friendship for All Seasons | 51

CONTENTS

13. Table Manners | 54
14. The Temple | 57
15. Traveling | 60
16. Disciples | 63

Part Three: **The Lion**

17. The Lion and the Lamb | 69
18. Vocation, Actually | 73
19. Losing One's Head | 76
20. Requests | 80
21. Questions | 83
22. Naked | 86
23. Relics | 89
24. Wild Beasts | 92

Part Four: **The Eagle**

25. Mystics in the Library | 97
26. Hell and How to Get There | 100
27. Who Needs the Incarnation? | 106
28. Why the Trinity? | 112
29. Why Care About the Eucharist? | 116
30. Where Is Heaven? | 120
31. Aging Gracefully | 126
32. Jesus and the Problem of Evil | 129

Endnotes | 135

Foreword

One of the questions that preoccupies me as a writer in an AI world is the value of human endeavor. What can humans write that AI can't? It seems to me that *Dying to See You!* offers us a good starting place. This is not to say that the students of St. Olaf's couldn't ask ChatGPT to write a tetramorphic suite of Chestertonian essays on the Four Gospels in the manner of Professor Taliaferro. Judging by the anecdotes in this book, they'd be more than capable of this. I doubt the results would either move or convince, though.

Dying to See You! has that unmistakable quality of human-made writing, rather like the thumbprints of the maker that are still visible on Wallace and Gromit figures. This collection offers a wealth of experience, erudition, and reflection, riffing on Gospel themes, posing questions, and simply relishing the stuff of life. The thinginess of things, the embodied nature of our lives; the glorious, the hilarious, the grave. "These essays are intended to be life-affirming," writes Taliaferro in his introduction. All manner of things are woven in, from the Eucharist, to a somersaulting dog, to a portrait stolen from a classroom wall. *Dying to See You!* comes from one human heart and mind to another—authentic, undefended. It's open-hearted, open-minded, and it is written in

FOREWORD

the unmistakable voice of the author. At times I snorted out loud, and at others, I was moved to tears.

I read the book sitting outdoors in the sunshine in late April in the UK. I was fighting off a bad cold, and I suddenly remembered sitting under the same patio umbrella at the same wrought iron table in a heatwave, while suffering from Covid in 2021. The shadow of Covid lies across some of these essays—would AI have come up with that? Would it have captured what it felt like to live through a global pandemic, how it reached into every corner of our lives? Would it know what it feels like to forgive and be forgiven, or be able to grasp the profound impact of small acts of kindness?

Dying to See You! knows all this and more. It offers a complex web of connections and unexpectedly juxtaposed material: ancient philosophers, the ransom theory of atonement, modern day Iran, "wild beast" academics, signs and parables, prison inmates-turned-philosophers, schoolboy arsonists, Narnia. This bright network of the imagination continues to grow in the reader's mind. As I coughed and read, I found myself making a strange connection to the Get Better Box my family had when I was a child. If you were poorly, you were given a decorated shoebox to play with. It was full of smaller boxes, containing little puzzles, toys, curious items like a tiny wooden apple with an even tinier tea set inside, pictures, miniature books, scraps of rich fabric, and so on. It came as a distraction, and as an acknowledgment that you were unwell and needed to be cherished. And, of course, it came with a wish that you would get better.

This book is a Get Better Box. It is full of unexpected treasures collected and offered to us by someone who cares. It's playful, and like the Balm of Gilead in the old hymn, "it cheers the sin-sick soul." It doesn't pretend that all is right with the world. There are chapters on death and hell. Taliaferro doesn't shy away from the dark stuff, whether that's a small pettiness he's detected in himself, or some large-scale evil: acts of terrorism and war atrocities. It breathes a wish throughout that the reader, the world, the cosmos will not only "get better"; it points beyond that to the eschatological hope that all things are being/will be gloriously recreated. And we are all surely dying to see that.

Dr. Catherine Wilcox/Catherine Fox

Manchester Metropolitan University

Acknowledgments

I am deeply grateful for the brilliant editing, advice, and encouragement of Kathleen Weflen. There have been many readers of earlier drafts, too many to name them all, but I especially thank Ann Bauleke, Karen Evans, ("Captain") Kirk Allison, Paul Reasoner, Jonathan Spence, Stephen Bilynsky, and Tom Erickson for their comments and encouragement. Tom has been a great comrade in our four years of weekly meetings in which we have (so far) read and discussed over five hundred essays. I am grateful for Calvin Jaffarian's expert preparation of the manuscript. Working with Cascade Books and Pickwick Publications editor Robin Parry is a delight. I am forever grateful for his expertise and support.

An Essential Introduction

I fell in love with light essays on life, love, and death in graduate school. It all started in a library in 1978.

It was a daybreak moment when I discovered the essays of G. K. Chesterton (1874–1936) in Harvard's Widener Library. Up until then I had a somewhat melancholic feeling about the library, despite its over three million books, as it is named in memory of a young Harvard graduate, Harry Widener (class of 1907), who perished along with his father in the 1912 sinking of the RMS *Titanic*. My melancholic preoccupation with that haunting tragedy in the North Atlantic Ocean (kindled by a portrait of Harry in which he seems to be looking at you) receded when I found effervescent, yet trenchant essays that made me laugh or smile, establishing a safe distance from the sometimes cut-and-thrust ethos of class and seminar rooms.

Graduate school was not exactly a constant martial affair, let alone a shipwreck—I found fantastic mentors and deeply satisfying collaborators—but I also felt overwhelmed by relentless critical evaluations and competition that left many of us gasping for air. Essays of Chesterton's like "The Thrill of Boredom," "A Defense of Rash Vows," "A Piece of Chalk," and "The Terror of a Toy" (some of which I memorized) kept me from drowning. Chesterton took everyday events (like finding some chalk to draw cows in the English

AN ESSENTIAL INTRODUCTION

countryside) and turned them into occasions of not just laughter but also exuberant wonder. Before I discovered his essays, I was developing a knack for the opposite: taking matters of exuberant wonder and turning them into everyday chalk.

Each of the essays in this book has been written in a Chestertonian spirit, though they presuppose no acquaintance with Chesterton. They are intended to be life-affirming. The reason for nailing my colors to the mast on this point is that I have wandered widely since my salad days among essay collections that are quite the opposite of life-affirming. An essay I read yesterday made me think it should come with one of those labels about the side-effects of amazing prescription drugs: Notify your doctor immediately if you start having suicidal thoughts. The essays in this book are all intended to be anti-suicidal. Yes, they address dying and death from various angles. There is even some reference to suicide, but the essays are intended to be buoyant rather than lead to self-harm. Whether you are agonizing in school or struggling mid-career or retired or happy-go-lucky at any age, I hope these essays provide the kind of amusing, philosophical sense of adventure I enjoyed in my twenties and continue to relish.

Some of Chesterton's essays were published in eclectic formats, as in *Tremendous Trifles* (1909) and *Alarms and Discursions* (1911). Some of his early, more organized collections had modest drawbacks as when his book *What's Wrong with the World* (1910) was published with a photograph of him on the cover, just under the title. Avoiding the eclectic and seeking a more nuanced format than Chesterton's book on the world's wrongs, I have organized the essays in this collection in accord with the tetramorph.

The *tetramorph* (Greek for *four shapes* or *forms*) refers to the four fantastic creatures who surround the throne of God in the book of Revelation. "The first living creature was like a lion, the second like an ox, the third had a face like a man, the fourth was like a flying eagle" (Rev 4:7; see also Ezek 1:10, which almost certainly inspired the vision in Revelations). Early and medieval Christians linked these living creatures with the four Gospels as well as with four spiritual perspectives. The human, who is sometimes depicted in Christian art with wings like an angel, is often taken to represent the beginning or the establishment of an orientation in the spiritual life. This human is associated with Matthew, whose Gospel opens with the genealogy of Jesus.

The ox, often thought of as a service animal and associated with sacrifice and redemption, is linked with Luke because his Gospel depicts the service of Jesus. Early Christians sometimes viewed the ox as a symbol of Christ. Many paintings and icons, as early as the fifth century, picture an ox along with an ass, or donkey, paying homage to Mary and Jesus.

The lion, associated with kingly power, majesty, strength, and courage, is linked to Mark, whose Gospel depicts Jesus as the Lion of Judah. The lion is also closely associated with Christ as the source of life, as it was once believed that young lions are born dead until breathed on by their sire. One can see this symbolic role of the breath of a lion in C. S. Lewis's *The Chronicles of Narnia*, in which the breath of Aslan plays a major role. And speaking of play, lions—like cats in general, and unlike dogs and many animals with claws—have retractable claws, allowing them to play without harm. Hence, Susan and Lucy play with Aslan in Narnia. In Christian lore the lion is the great protector, for it was believed that lions sleep with eyes open (akin to Ps 121:4).

The majestic soaring of the eagle is linked with John, whose Gospel begins with a transporting, awesome prelude of Jesus as divine. The eagle was also connected with the resurrection of Christ, as it was believed that the eagle renewed its plumage by flying close to the sun and then plunging into water. This legend of revitalizing may be in the background of Psalm 103:5, which says, "Thy youth is renewed like the eagle's." The eagle is sometimes inscribed in church lecterns, representing the inspiration of the gospel.

The four parts of this book are inspired by those four fantastic creatures. Part One, under the image of the winged human, addresses matters of orientation and beginnings. The essays draw on some elements of Matthew's Gospel, but they are best thought of as inspired by Matthean themes, rather than as an exposition of Matthew's Gospel. Part Two, under the symbol of the ox,

AN ESSENTIAL INTRODUCTION

proceeds with Lukan themes of service, sacrifice, and redemption. Part Three: The Lion contains essays involving different aspects of courage inspired, in part, by Mark's Gospel. Part Four: The Eagle is the most ambitious and dares to take up themes like the incarnation and Trinity.

I hope that this book, *Dying To See You!*, will inspire readers to engage the four Gospels, but it does not presuppose biblical literacy nor is it any kind of systematic biblical commentary. Instead, this book of playful essays on life, love, and death is loosely organized around the tetramorph as opposed to other arresting, fantastic biblical creatures or images like the skeleton army (Ezek 37:1), the four horsemen of the apocalypse (Rev 12:7), Leviathan (Job 41:18-19) or, a personal favorite, Balaam's ass (Num 22:23-35). Readers interested in such other imagery might enjoy the 2011 illustrated New International Version of the Bible with the subtitle *Incredible Creatures and Creations*.

Admittedly, depictions of the tetramorph are not as common as other Christian symbols, the cross or Madonna and child, for example, but it was of great interest to some outstanding early Christian theologians, including Irenaeus, Jerome, Ambrose, and Augustine. Actually, Jerome himself became closely associated with the lion, because of the story that an injured lion entered his monastery and Jerome healed him by removing a thorn from the lion's paw (as seen in many paintings, including the fifteenth-century work *St. Jerome Removing a Thorn from the Lion's Paw*, by Niccolo Antonio Colantonio). The tetramorph appears in the ninth-century Book of Kells. It is also depicted in sculpture in Chartres Cathedral and many other medieval churches.

AN ESSENTIAL INTRODUCTION

Image of Folio 27v from the ninth-century Book of Kells. The four winged creatures symbolize, top to bottom, left to right, Matthew, Mark, Luke, and John. Public domain.

The images may be making a comeback today. For example, the tetramorphic painting *Ezekiel's Vision* (ca. 1518), by Raphael, is reproduced as the cover image of Douglas Hedley's celebrated recent book *Living Forms of the Imagination*. You can even purchase tetramorph T-shirts online. As I am writing this introduction, I am drinking coffee from a mug that has this logo: *Got tetramorph?* The tetramorph symbol may not be ubiquitous, but it is not entirely Pickwickian, even if I currently look mildly eccentric typing this introduction in a coffeehouse wearing my tetramorph T-shirt. In my defense, I might look slightly less eccentric than Chesterton with his huge black cape, sword cane, crumpled hat, and cigar.[1]

Two more notes on the tetramorph: First, the perspectives of the human, ox, lion, and eagle can be interpreted as progressive stages in Christian spiritual life, akin to (but not correlating with) the widespread notion that Christian spirituality proceeds in three stages: illumination, purgation, and union (becoming united to or in harmony with God). However, unlike the three stages, the tetramorph need not be seen as an established sequence, just as the four Gospels need not be read sequentially. It may be that, as a very young person, one might begin with the eagle's point of view (John) and, as one ages, the human approach (Matthew) might be one's favored pathway. While I hope most readers will begin at the beginning of this book because the first chapters set the stage for what follows, skipping around this montage of essays would not be at all dangerous.

Second, while the tetramorph is only a loose demarcation into sets of themes, I believe that having a framework and connecting essays with Gospel themes is something that Chesterton would appreciate. In his autobiography, he wrote about his affection for frames and bridges:

> All my life I have loved frames and limits; and I will maintain that the largest wilderness looks larger when

---

1. On the tetramorph and other symbols: Gertrude Grace Sill, *A Handbook of Symbols in Christian Art* (New York: Simon & Schuster, 1975); George Ferguson, *Signs and Symbols in Christian Art* (Oxford: Oxford University Press, 1961).

seen through a window. . . . I have also a pretty taste in abysses and chasms and everything else that emphasizes a fine shade of distinction between one thing and another; and the warm affection I have always felt for bridges is connected with the fact that the dark and dizzy arch accentuates the chasm even more than the chasm itself.[2]

Speaking of frames and bridges, I found Chesterton himself to be a kind of frame or bridge as I transitioned from being a graduate student to becoming a professor. When I have encountered difficult moments with my own students over the years, such as when a student announced in a seminar on the philosophy of love that she hoped I would have a lifetime full of suffering and a pointless death, I would have "What would Chesterton do?" moments. Thanks to relying on Chesterton as a role model, I often (but not always) resist reactive defensiveness, and try to respond with a mixture of deep listening, self-deprecation, humor, and questions. I never found out what precisely motivated that student's position, but it didn't matter deeply because a year later, the (now) former student and I are friends, consoling each other with a heartfelt embrace at a recent memorial service for a mutual friend.

While such a resolution was beyond wonderful, I am especially grateful to the Chestertonian frame for a surprising reconciliation with a former student. At an international conference sponsored by the Vatican in Rome in the mid-1990s, a twenty-something-year-old graduate student approached me after his excellent presentation and said, "Professor, I owe you an apology."

Five years earlier, the student had come to my office with this rhetorical question: "Isn't your philosophical work discredited by the Enlightenment?" In a later conversation, he told me that assertion about my being discredited came from a professor in the religion department. (The professor was known for challenging conservative Christian students, using lines such as this: "Get it through your head: Jesus does not love you.") Anyhow, thanks to

---

2. G. K. Chesterton, *The Autobiography of G. K. Chesterton* (San Francisco: Ignatius, 2006), 41. For the complete work of G. K. Chesterton online, visit http://www.gkc.org.uk/gkc/books/.

AN ESSENTIAL INTRODUCTION

my resorting to a Chestertonian frame, my student and I had a good-humored exchange about the Enlightenment. He conceded that there was a chance that I had some credibility.

But, more importantly, years later in Rome, I accepted his (unnecessary) apology. While I was tempted to add that I thought the religion professor was wrong about Jesus (perhaps Jesus does love us all, including the religion professor), I thought it more fruitful to toast the young man's success as a scholar over a glass of wine.

In light of all this, I am tempted to add to the prayer for peace attributed to St. Francis: "Where there is hatred, let me sow love." Consider this variation: "When there are vexations in professor-student relations, help us to see things through Chesterton's capacious, resilient frame." The prayer might lead to finding reconciliation in a warm embrace, or to enjoying unexpected comradeship over a fine Italian wine at an international conference.

One other inspiration for this book deserves mention: Two students constructed something extraordinary for our class addressing Death and the Meaning of Life. I had invited the eminent philosopher Gordon Marino to address the class; his text was Søren Kierkegaard's essay "At a Graveside." Marino's presentation was brilliant and led me to hold our next class meeting at a graveyard. Bussing forty-some students to the nearest cemetery went smoothly, but my own presentation there was dubious. I recall running around in my academic, doctoral robes, quoting Kierkegaard, and saying, "We're all going to die."

Infinitely better than that graveyard moment, at the last meeting of the course, two students presented to the class a life-size coffin with passages from Kierkegaard's essay emblazoned on the inside of the coffin. A convenient reading light inside allowed students (and me) to get into the coffin to meditate on Kierkegaard's philosophy of life, death, and the love of God. Was it just a joke or an implied critique of my feckless role as a professor? The young carpenters (philosophy and religion majors) said they did the work to honor a positive, life-changing course. So, while not a joke or prank, it was certainly an extraordinary jest and gesture; it creatively combined wit with seriousness, a Chestertonian virtue. (When the students graduated, they left the coffin in the woods on campus. When campus security officers discovered it, they were utterly baffled, wondering if the college had fostered a morbid Kierkegaard cult.)

Because I have declared that these essays are written in a Chestertonian spirit, I should briefly underscore some similarities and dissimilarities between Chesterton and myself. Like Chesterton, I am Christian, but I have sought to avoid his occasional polemical writing about the superiority of his branch of Christianity, Roman Catholicism. For the record, I am an Anglican, or Episcopalian, who respects other communions and denominations (except for the rising tide in my country of Christian white nationalism), but in this book I have sought to avoid being parochial. I also seek to distance myself from Chesterton by using more inclusive language (avoiding lines like "every saint is a man before he is a saint") and especially avoiding any hint of anti-Semitism (alas, his otherwise hilarious drinking song "The Logical Vegetarian" is marred by its jarring third stanza).[3]

Chesterton did not include footnotes, but being a dyed-in-the wool scholar, I cannot resist adding either footnotes or endnotes to enable you to track down references and consider some further reading.

Finally, Chesterton was so prolific (four thousand essays, one hundred books, five novels, two hundred short stories, several hundred poems) that it is unlikely he did much revising or rewriting; there just would not have been enough time. My more modest work and time schedule has allowed me to revise each essay, as well as this introduction, countless times. I thank those dear souls who have improved these essays.

---

3. On saints: G. K. Chesterton, *Saint Thomas Aquinas* (New York: Image, 2013).
Chesterton's drinking song: "The Logical Vegetarian": https://www.chesterton.org/the-logical-vegetarian/.

Part One: The Winged Human

Chapter 1
Dying to See You!

My first publication on death did not go down very well. To understand why, you need to know about an advertising campaign for Guinness, an Irish dry stout. "Guinness is good for you" was a phrase coined in the early 1900s by the British detective writer, poet, and scholar Dorothy L. Sayers. The phrase became popular in the early 1990s, so much so that ads appeared in newspapers with a picture of a glass of Guinness with the words "Good for You" written above it. At the time of this Guinness campaign, I was asked to review a book for the *Times Literary Supplement*; the book was called *Confrontations with the Reaper: A Philosophical Study of the Nature and Value of Death*. I submitted a review with this suggested title: "Is Death Bad for You?" In the review I proposed that death is often very, very bad. Unfortunately, the *TLS* printed the review under the heading "Bad for You" and my name is printed just underneath. My plan to proudly share the review with my parents was shattered.[1]

While the phrase "Dying to see you!" can mean many things; it can simply be a dramatic, hyperbolic way of saying "I really, really want to see you." But it can also speak to this essay's theme. The Gospel of Matthew begins by earnestly establishing a framework,

PART ONE: THE WINGED HUMAN

a setting in which the life of Jesus is traced from birth to death. Needless to say, Jesus' death and resurrection are of monumental importance in that Gospel, but the majority of Matthew is taken up with Jesus' life. Matthew's Gospel is the only one in which the term *church* appears (16:18; 18:17); it ends with the resurrected Jesus' promise to be with his followers always, not just in their dying or death. I have come to experience a somewhat related shift: I still put a lot of weight on the importance of death and dying, but I've come to focus more on life and living. In a way, such a shift might even generate more gravity when I say to you that I'm dying to see you. This sentiment will take a little explaining.

As a professor of philosophy, when I would speak to either new or graduating students in my college, I would tell them that some of their professors will be giving, or have given, their all to them. Invariably, I would name some of the professors who died while they were professors, including some who taught under dire conditions and died shortly after they stopped teaching. This practice of acknowledging the dedication and death of professors led me to entertain a similar path for myself: I began to want to die in front of my students. I emphatically need to record that this was not a matter of self-harm! Rather, I imagined dying in the course of protecting students from harm or perhaps simply by me suffering a massive stroke. How great would it be if I had a heart attack, but just before death I would beckon students to love wisdom (the literal meaning of *philosophy* derived from the term for love, *philo*, and wisdom, *sophia*) or to urge students to become philosophy majors? This desire for a kind of heroic, or at least memorable, death may have been enhanced by my teaching heroic texts like Herodotus's depiction of the Battle of Thermopylae, when three hundred Spartans made a last stand against a vast, invading Persian army in the fifth century BCE. Imagine 300 Spartans facing an army estimated at 120,000 to 300,000 soldiers! I came to valorize the glory (*kleos* in Greek) that would be mine if I died protecting my students, just as Leonidas protected mainland Greece.[2]

Fortunately, my view has changed for three major reasons.

First off, I realized that I had to be pretty pathetic as a professor if the best way I could imagine to teach or to get the attention of my students was to die in front of them. Surely, it would be far easier to die in class than to actually do the hard work of preparing a rewarding lecture or create a lively dialogue. Gradually, the whole macabre fantasy of dying like King Leonidas turned pallid. Of course, I persist in hoping that if my classroom were invaded by a Persian army, I would not be a coward, but this is different from hoping that the invasion would take place.

Second, guessing that I had a vainglorious fantasy, my students teased me mercilessly. Perhaps they saw through me when I would tear up retelling the Battle of Thermopylae when a brave Spartan, Dienekes, replied to the enemy's claim that they would fill the sky with so any arrows, it would block out the sun: "Very well, we'll fight in the shade." For several days, I was hammered with humiliating "gifts." Some students created a fake newspaper with a photoshopped picture of me dying after rescuing children from a burning bus. It had this headline: "Professor Finally Achieves Kleos as He Perishes Heroically in a Petroleum-Based Fire."

Inspired by a report that older mice were rejuvenated by an injection of blood from young mice, a student (assisted by his physician parents) drew a vial of his own blood and gave it to me in case I needed extra fortitude in fighting evil. "It's funny, but it didn't taste that strange," I told the class, though in fact I did not drink it, but disposed of it in a biohazard can.

Even more dramatic, one day in class two students appeared to get into a fight. It took a few minutes before I realized this was "fantasy violence," and they expected me to "heroically" break it up. As I separated the "fighters," the laughter (at me) was clamorous. In any case, with a little help from my students, my desire to be a better professor began eclipsing my desire to be a dying professor.

The third, most serious reason for my change of focus involved a mother, Kate, and her son Rick (I have changed their names to protect privacy). Rick was a great student-athlete, but he suffered from crippling shyness and exceptionally low self-esteem. His speech was halting; it also did not help that he felt like an outsider as a Black student in a predominantly White school, which was slowly diversifying. Kate, an artist, was friends with my wife, Jil, so I got to know her off campus.

PART ONE: THE WINGED HUMAN

Kate and I stood together in a parking lot as she told me she had a brain tumor and less than a year to live. She asked me, crying, to look after Rick. I cried as well. We embraced.

I did look after Rick in three classes, working with his confidence as a writer and speaker, doing what I could, however awkwardly, to encourage his sense of belonging to our college. What really fueled Rick's eventual flourishing was not my pedagogy, but the indissoluble, evident love of his mother, as well as the loving encouragement of his father and brothers. It was clear that Kate wished Rick and others joy. Even when she cried, she had a smile that was radiant. Kate was a person of faith, and while she took the reality of her immanent death seriously, she was firmly on the side of loving life and living. In that light, two months before Kate died, she sponsored a one-week holiday for her family in Hawaii.

There was no question that Kate's death was bad for her and her family and for those who, like me, came to love her. Yet, what she taught me was that it was not her dying that made a difference to Rick and to the rest of us. It was her contagious love. She wanted Rick and those around her to live life to the full with joy. As far as Kate's family was concerned, Kate was all in to the end, without reservations. And if there is life after this life, I wager that her love continues.

Kate may or may not have taken heart from St. Matthew, but his Gospel too stresses the ongoing love and life of Jesus, a life and love that is stronger than death.

Now, if I tell you *I am dying to see you*, I don't mean that *I fervently hope you see me dying in the course of rescuing you from peril*. For all sorts of reasons, such a dysfunctional, misplaced desire for attention is—to use British slang—simply not on. Of course, I am saying, as the expression usually means, I really, really want to see you. But thanks to Kate, I now mean something more. In the spirit of a mother's profound love for her son, I also mean that I really want to see you living life to the full with joy.

I'm all in. No reservations.

Chapter 2
Repairing the World

In Matthew's Gospel, the phrases *kingdom of God* and *kingdom of heaven* occur thirty-five times. We are told that the kingdom of heaven is at hand (10:7). The kingdom of heaven is said to belong to children (19:14). We are taught to pray for the coming of God's kingdom (6:10).

Growing up, I did not have misgivings about kings and kingdoms. Aragorn was a good king in Tolkien's Middle-Earth, and the kings and queens in Narnia seemed relatable. Images of King Arthur and the knights of the Round Table were in our home, since we inherited Arthurian artwork by the American illustrator Howard Pyle, a distant relation. But I gradually came to realize that glimpses of a heavenly kingdom were periodic and sometimes occurred in ordinary acts—what is called *tikkun olam* in Hebrew, repairing the world—rather than with knights and their horses, armor, and pageantry.

As a boy, it became very clear to me that God's kingdom was not (at least at first glance) at the all-male boarding school I was sent to when I was thirteen. I was certainly not sent to Camelot. William Golding's 1954 novel, *The Lord of the Flies*, captures something of my sense of being a pupil in that school.

PART ONE: THE WINGED HUMAN

My school was filled to the brim with bullying, some of which was bizarre. When playing sports, my roommate would growl at me. He seemed to transform himself into a mad dog. Some of the assaults in the dorm were bloody, though not lethal. And the arson bordered on the apocalyptic. In 1967 several of my classmates set fire to three of our teachers' cars. I still recall vividly the explosions and three columns of flames arising from the parking lot. My ninth-grade peers then burned down a chapel built by Native Americans and gifted to our school. I was quite certain that I was not witnessing God's kingdom. More likely, I was witnessing attempts to rip apart the world.

In retrospect, I came to see that the assaults and fires were less severe than I experienced them. But at the time, these events shook me to the core; they occurred in an unlikely place, an expensive prep school, and the arsonists were children of wealthy parents. Still, in the midst of such mayhem, I might have caught a glimpse of God's kingdom, or at least a glimpse of something other than the killing of Piggy in Golding's dystopian book.

On the night of the arson, I made my way to the main school chapel and prayed aloud for all the boys involved. I cried. I am sure I said I loved Roger, John, and so on, naming names. I then heard laughing from behind the altar. The arsonists had gotten to the chapel before I arrived; they'd come to drink the wine that was to be used for communion. Their laughter chilled me to the bone. I thought: I am dead. I will be sliced to the bone.

When I returned to my dormitory, there was no bullying. Not even teasing. Nor derisive laughter. Of course, this may have been due to the presence of firefighters, police, proctors, and faculty. But I like to believe that my unbridled crying and profession of love may also have given the boys pause. Probably not. But I don't regret trying to reach God during the trauma.

A second incident at school was formative, and the opposite of the night of ripping apart the world with fire. In the eleventh grade, my peers and I were swimming off a barrier beach on Florida's east coast. Two of us got caught in a riptide; the powerful current carried us offshore. We tried to swim against it, but made no progress at all. (I learned later that riptides can extend as far as 980 feet, and every year in the United States, some one hundred people die from rip currents.) My friend and I started to panic. In the nick of time, we were rescued by boys on surfboards who swam across the riptide, escaping its deadly, ebbing force. I thanked heaven for this deliverance. Of course, I also thanked my rescuer and was relieved that not all boys in boarding school were servants of Beelzebub, the devil described in antiquity as the lord of flies.

I think it was these experiences, among others, that shaped my Christian faith as I reached draft age during the last phase of the war in Vietnam, which did not end until the fall of Saigon in 1975. I registered as a conscientious objector, citing the radical teaching of nonviolence by Jesus in Matthew's depiction of the Sermon on the Mount. In that sermon, we are implored to turn the other cheek, to love rather than to hate. I wanted to be like the boys who rescued those of us at risk of drowning. I certainly did not want to kill fellow human beings in Vietnam, Laos, and Cambodia. Two of my brothers served in the U.S. Army in the war and came home with eyewitness testimony of atrocities that made my experience of violence in prep school look like a garden party. As it turns out, my lottery number was high, and so I was not drafted for alternative service in a government-approved, nonmilitary institution, such as a hospital, nursing home, or halfway house.

Over the years, I still catch a glimpse of heaven here and there, quite apart from dramatic events like expressing love for student-arsonists or near drowning experiences or even trying to protest what many of us thought was an unjust war in Southeast Asia. The Christian philosopher Charles Taylor writes about how minor, nondramatic acts on behalf of the good can be profound. Healing, sacred acts can take place on a small, personal scale, in which we can distance ourselves from the world's titanic amount of evil. He writes:

> There is also a positive response to this [the world's ills]; when you feel able to act, to do something to heal the world; when you can feel part of the solution and not

simply part of the problem. We can have this sense from acting on a small scale, feeling that we are upholding our end in our immediate surroundings, and therefore doing our bit to *tikkun olam*, to use the pithy Hebrew expression, which we might render as "healing the world."[3]

I end this essay by recounting an incident of *tikkun olam*. This was not a case of high drama, but it seemed to reflect the kind of concrete act of love enjoined by Jesus in the Sermon on the Mount. The principle agents of love who showed my wife and me something of God's kingdom were a mother and daughter, both Muslims. (Incidentally, the Qur'an has abundant verses about being peacemakers, the kingdom of heaven, aiding others out of love for Allah; and with ninety verses about Jesus, that sacred book is not reluctant about recognizing Jesus' prophetic mission. More on Islam in another essay.)

One afternoon, Jil and I were in a traffic accident. A van ran a red light and hit our car broadside. It was a hit-and-run event, as the van left the scene at top speed. We were not physically injured, but shocked and destabilized. We extracted ourselves from our car, then called the police and a tow truck. The circumstances were particularly stressful as our city, Minneapolis, had just seen serious rioting after the killing of George Floyd, an unarmed African American, by a police officer on May 25, 2020. The pharmacy and gas station near our home had been burned down. What's more, we were in the pandemic. So, there was tension in the air, but the kindness shown to us at the time was personal, small-scale, and wonderful.

A mother and her daughter stopped their car and came to our side. They wore traditional African-Muslim clothing of bright yellow and green. They stood in solidarity with us for about an hour until the police arrived, only leaving us briefly to purchase bottled water for us. They consoled us when we were disoriented and vulnerable. We even shared some good humor when we discovered that when the van hit us, its license plate was dislodged. When the police asked us if we had seen and remembered the license number of the van, we simply handed over the license plate. "It doesn't get any better than this," the officer commented.

In any event, what that Muslim mother and daughter did for us shines as you take into account the sometimes-hostile treatment of the Muslim community in Minneapolis. The Mercy Islamic Center had been set on fire twice. The Dar al-Farooq Islamic Center was bombed. And yet, this kind pair of Muslims stood with us. The mother and daughter did not accept our offer to pay for the water or to pay for something more, such as dinner for their whole family. I did not ask, but the daughter may have been the same age as I was during the arson in boarding school. I was in awe of her kindness. Her mother said they got us water because her daughter thought we looked tired and thirsty.

Maybe the kingdom of heaven can surprise us, coming into view not only in some dramatic events, but also in smaller-scale events in which a part of the world, however small, is unexpectedly healed. At a time when the national and international news agencies were covering the deployment of the National Guard in our city, they missed out on something we witnessed: a blazing instance of *tikkun olam* or, in Arabic, *ishlah*.

Chapter 3

Homeward Bound

> (An earlier version of this essay was written for students at St. Olaf College, near graduation. It is in accord with Matthew 7:24–27 on the importance of building a house on a rock, rather than on sand.)

Probably few students think of their education as a matter of coming home. There are a dizzying number of other images that seem more apt: a college education can be regarded as an adventure, a means to a career, self-discovery; it can involve experiments with relationships (ranging from the ecstatic to the catastrophic), sports, recreational substances, and international travel (a specialty of my college), and so on. But I suggest that a large and vital part of education is finding a way to be at home with yourself.

You are likely aware of the description of someone who kind of sleepwalks through life: the lights are on, but no one is at home. Being at home with who and what you are is not easy. It is all too tempting to not inhabit what you say and instead to speak in clichés, tell white lies, and repeat popular sentiments.

I believe that we can be self-estranged too often, more happy or comfortable with illusions or delusions of who we are. Along those lines, one of my biggest fears is self-deception. I claim to believe lots of things and am often greatly relieved when occasions reveal that I am not fooling myself: For example, I claim to love teaching at St. Olaf College, but I grew in my confidence in that claim when I turned down two attractive job offers elsewhere.

Many ethical and religious traditions prohibit lying to others. I am not doubting such teachings, but I propose that the most damaging form of lying is lying to yourself. Obviously, I am not the first to point this out. The Danish existentialist philosopher Søren Kierkegaard railed against complacent, inauthentic living. One of the problems of lying to yourself is that you can become your own prisoner, both victim and victimizer. Just as liars to other people risk losing their grasp of what is true, I suggest things are even worse when you are both the liar and the one being lied to.

The importance of being at home with yourself, of self-integration, has become enhanced for me in recent years as I have balanced being a liberal arts professor with working with prisoners. Some of my books have found their way into several prison libraries in the United States. Some of my book titles, such as *The History of Evil* and *A Companion to Evil*, might have particular appeal to those charged with breaking laws. As a result of extensive correspondence, I now have several friends serving terms, including life sentences without parole. Because COVID prevented my teaching in person in prison and the prisoners I work with have no access to computers, communication has been epistolary (carried on by letters in US mail). A fellow philosophy professor and I helped one prisoner get his "A Prison Philosopher: A Personal Essay" published in a good philosophy journal.[4]

All of this work with people in prison has made me in awe of the immense task of personal reform, of coming to terms with the past (often involving murder) and building a sense of unity, being a whole person, renewed by helping fellow prisoners, reaching out to their own families, seeking forgiveness, and offering restitution. Some of my incarcerated friends are fighting hard against self-deception and have thrown themselves into building up a sense of themselves with practical wisdom (the Greek term is *phronesis*) and virtue.

My hope and prayer for my students (and myself), incarcerated or free, is that we find integrity as ourselves, as whole persons, being at home with ourselves, rather than fragmented and torn by internal divisions.

So, I ask students, what are you doing after graduation? Medical school? Law school? Teach For America? Science or the arts? In my view, a good answer to such a question is this: I'm homeward bound.

Chapter 4
In the Beginning

From time to time, I can slip into escapist literature or daydreaming and wind up in Narnia or Middle-Earth. Finding the path back to my somewhat less magical life (where, if I run into a dragon, it's a metaphor) is not always easy. After some binge reading of Tolkien's short stories on my way to a job interview, I had to review my own résumé so that I could play the proper role of who I am in this world, rather than imagining I was some kind of elf living in Rivendell. Fantasy and real life strayed dangerously close one year when a Christian Tolkien-oriented group, called the Rivendell Institute, invited me to lecture at Yale University. The thought occurred to me that maybe there is a Rivendell in this world, after all.

I might have picked up the habit of reminding myself of my real identity from my mother, Margaret Taliaferro, who wrote a book titled *In the Beginning*, which paraphrased the Old Testament for children.[5] It is a radiant, conversational text by someone who taught Sunday school with magical demonstrations, such as turning water into wine, to illustrate stories. She appeared to do such a miracle by showing the kids a pitcher of water and then stirring in a spoonful of red food dye. She illustrated the story of the three young men in a pit of fire (Dan 3:8–25) by wrapping toy soldiers in silver foil and then putting them onto a charcoal fire.

She made praying fun. I remember her bringing a globe to class. We would take turns spinning it until one of us stopped it by pointing to a place. We would then pray for the children living there. I am not sure the children of Iceland benefited from our prayers, but maybe some did.

My mother brought that kind of sense of play and imagination into her writing. And what stuck in my mind as a boy and remains now is the idea of the importance of remembering the beginning of things, whether this was a matter of a theological supposition—recalling God as creator—or the beginning of my life, the beginning of various life episodes such as relationships and jobs, or even the beginning of a dinner party. The ancient Greek philosopher Aristotle once observed that a work that is begun well is half completed: "Well begun is half done." Christian spiritual tradition sometimes stresses the importance of the beginning with the precept that we should return to the source of life; we should journey *ad fontes* (Latin for "to the sources") or, since God is likened to "the fountain of living waters" in Jeremiah (2:13; 17:13), *ad fontem* ("to the fountain").

Many of us look for signs, or symbols, to represent and guide parts of our lives. I often represent my life around some (awkwardly drawn) symbols. Some of the more enduring ones are an ox, a lion, a fountain, a giraffe, a dolphin, and the Greek initials for alpha and omega. The giraffe, for example, represents Platonism, perhaps because I believe Plato helps one see far. The alpha and omega stem from Jesus' declaration of being the Alpha and Omega (Rev 22:13–15), the beginning and the end.

The dolphin made an appearance while I was visiting my mother in Florida when she was receiving nursing care at home. She lived on a barrier reef island on the east coast. In between times of reading to her, I walked along the intracoastal waterway where I saw dolphins heading south, bobbing up and down in the water. In ancient history and mythology, dolphins have symbolized harmony, cooperation, and peace. For Christians, when the image of a dolphin is paired with an anchor (a symbol of salvation), it can stand for controlled speed or prudence, and when combined with a trident it can symbolize the crucifixion. The Greek historian Herodotus tells the delightful story of a minstrel, Arion, being saved by a dolphin. I was quite sure that the dolphins were not going to attempt to save my mother, but their presence so near her home lifted my spirits.

When my mother passed away in October 2010, I half expected a sign. I wasn't sure what kind of sign. From her? Not impossible. If a sign appeared, it would be subtle and humorous. While flying home after the memorial service, I looked again at the church bulletin and laughed. On the cover is a picture of Mom standing by the boat she and my father loved. It looks like dawn. My mother is holding up the dinghy. The inflatable rubber dinghy is collapsed into the shape of the Greek letter *alpha*, A, the sign for beginning.

My secular colleagues expect me as a professional philosopher to not be superstitious or believe in magic or miracles. But what if death is not the absolute end for us and some signs of the divine are not to be ruled out? Maybe Jesus once did turn water into wine, for example. Putting to one side secular misgivings and adopting a more receptive perspective, I don't think it's preposterous to think that this dinghy *alpha* image was the kind of sign my mother would send. In any event, it made me laugh. Not in a shy way, but a laughter like Frodo and Sam from *The Lord of the Rings* shared on their way to Mordor. Frodo "laughed a long clear laugh from his heart. Such a sound had not been heard in those places since Sauron came to Middle-Earth."[6]

Chapter 5

Parables and Parabolic Performances

The Gospel of Matthew has a cornucopia of parables. There is the parable of the sower, the treasure in the field, the pearl of great price, the dragnet, the unforgiving servant, the workers in the vineyard, the wicked tenants, the ten maidens, and more. Parables are stories that convey some teaching or insight based on analogies or examples. So, the parable of the sower conveys the different ways in which God's word or revelation may be received. Jesus uses a commonplace farming practice to convey the importance of receiving God's word without being stifled by the worries of this world. Parables can involve a reframing of current events in order to expose underlying values or assumptions.[7]

Probably the most famous biblical case of using a parable to expose wrong occurs when the prophet Nathan confronts King David over his adultery with Bathsheba and arranging for her husband, Uriah, to be killed in battle (2 Sam 12). Nathan presents David with a story about a rich man who exploits a poor man, stealing his lamb and killing it for his own pleasure. David is enraged and declares that the wealthy man is to be condemned.

Nathan then says simply: "You are the man." David's sin is exposed and he is led to grave repentance.

I have learned many parables outside the Old and New Testaments. Real events can assume the role of a parable, such as the sinking of the *Titanic*. The comic newspaper *The Onion* used this parable humorously. Its main article refers to the White Star Line vessel as "the world's largest symbol of man's mortality and vulnerability." The ship, named after the Greek gods the Titans, and its fateful sinking continue to stand for the way in which human hubris can be disastrous. Of course, there is nothing merely symbolic or metaphorical about the more than fifteen hundred lives lost, but as evidence that the term *titanic* carries symbolic weight, I note an edit of a recent co-authored chapter. I suggested we begin the chapter with this line: "Theism has had a titanic impact on the history of philosophy." My co-author replied, "As a British subject, I prefer we not use the term *titanic*."

More recently than biblical times and the sinking of the *Titanic*, I have learned from what may be called the parabolic performances of my students. I cite one case that involves not exactly the exposure of a sin like David's, but one that addresses the vice or fault of a liberal arts professor and offers some kind of consolation.

Some background is essential. One day, I was having an awful time in class. I was perhaps thrown off by two visitors, a dean from another school and his daughter, a prospective student. "Professor," a student asked, "can psychotropic drugs enhance religious experiences?" I vaguely recall mumbling something about Aldous Huxley. My plan or expectation for a profound dialogue crumbled. Class discussion got worse and worse as I tried to make some point about probability theory. Several students disagreed. What was worrisome was that I realized that those who disagreed with me were brilliant. They had acumen, whereas in comparison I had prattle. Two things then happened in quick succession. First, I found myself saying, "Of course I'm right. I have a PhD." And almost simultaneously, I realized I was wrong. The students were right. All I could do at the time was surrender and confess. The whole class heard me yell: *"I am not an idiot!"*

I underscored my admission the next time the class met. I started out by writing on the backboard *"I am an idiot"* and then I bashed my head against the board. There was no blood, but it hurt and was loud. In any case, the class got back on track (or so it seemed). Thank heavens, the class seemed to have buoyancy and energy and a generous spirit.

Now for the parabolic performance. At the end of the term, the students requested time for a performance. The event began with two students dressed up like demons. They were talking about going to Earth in order to haunt a liberal arts professor. They decided to appear as a dean and his daughter. Coming to planet Earth, they approached a student dressed up to look like me. He had my mannerisms; he had white disheveled hair; he wore an orange watch, untucked shirt, loose tie, and so on. After tormenting him with awkward questions, the "professor" wrote on the blackboard "I am an idiot" and then smashed his head into the board. We all laughed.

There is a biblical saying that "love covers a multitude of sins" (1 Pet 4:8). I am not sure what that means, but the takeaway from that parabolic performance was probably not just *Beware of demons* (although the hypothesis that the hideous class was due to supernatural evil agents did give me a defense). The lesson was probably closer to that line about love. For me, one of the lessons of that parabolic performance is something like this: *Sometimes, laughter, affection, and a playful imagination can console and firm-up a professor's resolution to mortify any vain pretensions in the future.* I may still be an idiot from time to time, but with the aid of some of my students, I vowed to avoid such ghastly disasters in future classes.

I cannot resist describing one more student parabolic performance due to its extraordinary imagination and its confronting a fundamental assumption on college campuses. This performance took place in a philosophy class in which we discussed the nature of time and any possible limits to God's omnipotent power. We read a medieval text that took up the question of whether God could restore a person's virginity. Erik asked for some time at the end of class for a performance.

Erik, wearing lab coat, began by unveiling a complex device he described as a "re-virginerizer machine." He turned the machine on, with its lights and mechanical noises. He asked for a student volunteer who was not a virgin but would like to have virginity restored. A male student eagerly came forward. He assumed a chair and Erik attached him to the machine. Lights flashed and there was mechanical noise. After a minute, Erik declared him a virgin. The student immediately called his mother with the good news. Erik then gave a five-minute presentation on the beauty and value of virginity. Everyone in class was shocked. Was he being ironic or serious? Not sure either way, we all clapped, Erik bowed, and the performance was over. I gave him an A+.

About a year later, I ran into Erik and asked him whether his case for virginity was serious or ironic. "Serious," he said. "And to anticipate your next question you dare not ask, I am a virgin, but I am getting married next month. And I am very excited."

Probably no unpacking of the parabolic performance is necessary, but I note its effectiveness. Erik's case for virginity was not on the assumption that sexual intercourse was abominable. He did not make a case for the glory of celibacy. Nor was he making the obvious point that sometimes sexual intercourse can be wrong or regrettable (when it involves deception and so on). He was, rather, challenging an assumption that is probably prevalent on most college campuses today: Virginity is not valuable. On the contrary, sexual activity is frequently taken to be a sign of maturity, competence, and perhaps some kind of glory. In my view, Erik's performance was an extraordinary way of challenging a common, social assumption. He used humor and farce to articulate a neglected good.

Agreed, my students' parabolic performances aren't on the level of the use Nathan makes of a parable to expose the sin of a king. Indeed, Nathan's prophetic work was so momentous in exposing David's sin of adultery and murder that its truth is hauntingly sewn into the genealogy of the Gospel of Matthew. The mother of

Solomon is referred to as "Uriah's wife" (Matt 1:6). But while my students have yet to equal Nathan's (perhaps God-given) wisdom, they have certainly outpaced my occasional colossal faults.

Chapter 6
Ransom

In the Gospel of Matthew, Jesus refers to himself as a ransom. He says he "did not come to be served, but to serve, and to give his life as a ransom for many" (Matt 20:28). There are multiple accounts of how the life of Jesus (his birth, teachings, miracles, suffering, death, and resurrection) brings about our atonement (at-one-ment) with God. These include accounts about how Jesus bore the punishment that we deserve for sin, how Jesus saves us through suffering, and how Jesus saves us by embodying the love of God and thus providing a moral and spiritual exemplar for us to follow. Among these theories, there is also what is known as the ransom theory. I offer a brief sketch of the theory and some reasons why it is more viable than its critics, past and present, admit.

In a nutshell, according to one early version of the ransom theory, human beings, through sin or evildoing, became captive of the devil. In some versions, we became captive to sin, the devil, and death. In order to free us, Jesus Christ (fully God and fully human) was offered as a ransom for our release. The devil agreed to this exchange, but when the exchange was made and Jesus was handed over through his suffering and death, Jesus defeated the devil (or the threefold enemy of sin, devil, and death) by his resurrection from the dead. With some variations, important early Christians like Origen, Maximus the Confessor, and Gregory of Nyssa accepted this theory or model.

The objections to this view are legion. Here are five: (1) It gives the devil too much of a role in our atonement. (2) Even if there is a devil, wouldn't it be unethical to negotiate with the devil? Today we hear from some that they will not negotiate with terrorists as it implicitly involves recognizing the authority of terrorists. (3) Even if negotiation with the devil is permissible, doesn't this theory implicate Jesus or God in deception? Surely, that is unfitting of God as a supremely good being. (4) By what means does Jesus or God liberate us from our captivity? This liberation seems very different from more straightforward cases of recovering kidnapped persons by paying money or ceding some political goal. Why not just overpower the devil and pull off a liberation without making any payment? (5) Sin and evildoing have continued occurring long after Jesus' resurrection. Jesus' atoning work to free us from a cosmic hostage crisis seems pretty ineffectual.

It would take a whole book to do justice to these objections. Fortunately, I have written such a book.[8] In this essay, I offer a few replies to the objections in order to encourage you to not dismiss the theory outright.

(1) Admittedly, the theory may be too supernatural for many modern Christians. Sure, the devil (and demons) appear in the New Testament, but none of the creeds of the church involve professing to believe that the devil exists. Christians today often discount the prevalence through Christian history of the belief in the devil, but I offer to skeptics a possible revision of the theory in which the devil is taken to be a metaphor or symbol of the nature of sin and evil. Doesn't some sin and evildoing at least feel like a kind of captivity? Perhaps this is more evident in cases of addiction when an addict can feel enslaved to the object of addiction (alcohol, drugs). But doesn't such an enslavement also make sense when a person is held captive by vanity, resentment, rage, greed, vindictive passions? And victims of evil acts can certainly feel captive and be held captive. Domestic abuse, for example.

(2) Is negotiating with the devil (real, supernatural, or metaphor) always wrong? This is not obvious to me. Sometimes a negotiator can free hostages by exposing the futility of the hostage-taking, or a negotiator can deploy a strategy to liberate the captives by an exchange that will defeat the hostage-takers. Remember, too, some versions of the ransom theory see us as willing hostages. If we have a case of Stockholm syndrome, we need to be talked into leaving our captivity. Christ offering of himself as a loving, wise, awesome ransom might do something to break the spell of captivity.

(3) Some defenders of the ransom theory thought it would not be wrong for Jesus or God to deceive the devil. This is why the ransom theory has sometimes been called the mousetrap theory. In this vein, Jesus is akin to the cheese, placed in a way to lure the devil into the trap. I personally do not have a problem with such a scenario. Deception is not always wrong. In World War II when the Allies deceived the Germans into thinking that the Allies were not invading occupied France at Normandy, were they wrong? I doubt it.

For examples of when deception is wicked, or not just benign, but used as an instrument for justice and reconciliation, I recommend taking into account some of Shakespeare's plays. Deception is employed for wicked, murderous means in *Othello* (Iago uses deception to drive Othello into killing his faithful, loving wife, Desdemona), in *Cymbeline* (Iachimo deceives Posthumus into ordering Pisanio to kill Innogen on the wrongful assumption that Innogen has been unfaithful to him), and in *Macbeth* (Macbeth and Lady Macbeth deceive the king of Scotland into believing he is safe in their castle). But deception is used for the good to expose vice in *Measure for Measure* (the duke, disguised as a friar, exposes the wickedness of Angelo and brings about reconciliation in his kingdom), and in *Twelfth Night* deception is used for ending the grief and emotional sterility of the seaport city of Illyria (Viola, a woman disguised as a male page, Cesario, plays a role in Olivia's recovery from grieving the death of her brother and dispelling the melancholy of the duke). And in some plays, characters are deceived into thinking they have killed someone they once loved, but they are led to repentance and reconciliation when the one presumed to have been killed is revealed to be alive. In *The Winter's Tale*, a repentant King Leontes reconciles with his wife, Queen Hermione, when she appears to him alive long after he thought he had caused her death. *Much Ado About Nothing*, *The Tempest*, and others are examples of when characters are deceived into thinking a dear one is dead but later shown to be alive. These plays may hint at the Christian motif of *how renewed life overcomes sin and death*, albeit Christians believe there was no deception in the claim that Christ actually died and then came back to life.[9]

Another reply to the deception objection on behalf of the ransom theory is to claim that no deception of any kind is involved between Jesus and Satan. After all, in Matthew's Gospel, Jesus foretells his death and resurrection (16:21). We can imagine Satan (whether real or a metaphorical figure) is skeptical about Jesus' power to overcome sin and death, but presumably the fault would not lie with Jesus being deceptive. Perhaps Satan's skepticism was akin to that of some scholars today who are skeptical of the historical reliability of the New Testament. I am not implying that such skeptics are satanic! I am simply pointing out that it is possible that Satan, like some New Testament scholars, may not have believed Jesus' foretelling his resurrection. Most likely, such contemporary scholars do not believe in the existence of evil supernatural agents like Satan and other demons. I am 100 percent convinced they do not seek to serve Satan (whether real or a metaphor). In any case, I suggest that the deception objection to the ransom theory is not at all decisive.

(4) So, by what means does Jesus liberate the captives? Advocates of the theory stress that the liberation occurs through Jesus' resurrection in which he promises new, transformed life to repentant wrongdoers and victims. It is nothing like a monetary exchange, but it is an exchange. If sin, evil, and death are intertwined, why not think of being free of them through the goodness of Jesus, as he overcomes evil and death by resurrection? As for the option of Jesus or God not paying a ransom, this overlooks

what early defenders of the theory held. In the ransom theory, we human beings willfully gave ourselves over to captivity. To free captives from a jail, it is not enough to break down the gates. One must convince the prisoners to walk out of prison. By Jesus' courageous birth, teaching, miracles, suffering, death, and resurrection, he inspires us to get out of our captivity.

(5) All accounts of the atonement between God and humans need to address the fact that sin and death—and the devil, if there is one—remain very much in evidence since the life and resurrection of Jesus. What the ransom theory offers is a framework in which each person and community since the earthly life of Jesus can take heart in aligning in solidarity with Jesus in being purged from sin and evil and finding life in him in this world and, by God's grace, in the next.

All of the above needs to be filled out, and some other essays in this collection will do so. All this essay is intended to do is to at least stall the ransom theory's being cast aside as obviously untenable. The standard for what makes a good argument philosophically, or theologically, is highly contentious these days. I am sympathetic with a colleague when he says that he counts it a great success if, after making a presentation, a peer responds: "Well, maybe." That is what I am aiming for with you.

I end on a conciliatory note: As I argue elsewhere, the ransom theory need not displace alternative accounts of atonement. Perhaps some judicial account of the atonement is plausible in which Christ suffers in our place for our guilt. In Charles Dickens's *A Tale of Two Cities*, Sydney Carton, an innocent man, sacrifices his life for the sinful Charles Darnay. You can accept such a penal substitution model (an innocent person pays the ultimate penalty for the guilty) and yet believe the price paid by Christ was *also* a ransom, a costly rescue to set persons free from sin, death, and the devil. In this realm of theology, more than one model can be explanatory, just as there is more than one explanation for my writing this book and your reading it. Reasoning in theology and philosophy can be more like binding together many different strands to make a rope, rather than forging links to make a single chain (which is only as strong as its weakest link).

Chapter 7

Prayer Times

The Lord's Prayer appears in the Gospel of Matthew 6:9–13. The Lord's Prayer can be rattled off in a routine way or it can be a virtual banquet of wisdom or, changing metaphors, it can function as a mode to intentionally seek concord in the presence of God (*Coram Deo* in Latin). Sometimes, the prayer is taken to be an elementary first prayer, perhaps something to teach children. That idea was in play when my family went skiing in Vermont. When we were young, we children were instructed to ski on a hill called "The Lord's Prayer," until we were older and skilled enough to ski down mountains.

In this essay, I want to engage in something more fundamental, namely to address obstacles not just to saying the Lord's Prayer, but also to saying any prayers at all.

So, I hope you will join me in considering several obstacles to the practice of prayer, beginning with the charge that praying to God who is believed to be omniscient and unsurpassably good is pointless. Doesn't God already know your true desires, your inmost thoughts, your vices and virtues?

Good point. It is perhaps in light of those considerations that some religious believers give primacy to silent prayer. But part of the point of prayer is for us to put into language what are our desires, our inmost thoughts, our vices and virtues. If you are like me, you may need to express verbally or to write out your thoughts and feelings to discover or confirm them. I become more present to you, and you to me, to the extent that we can share in language—including body language—who we are.

Augustine argued that prayer can be a relational experience between persons and between persons and God. And prayer can significantly speak to the relationship between ourselves and our bodies. In the church I belong to, confession before a priest is recommended but not required. There are two related sayings about confession. One says: *Confession is recommended to all, required of none, but strongly recommended to some.* The other says: *All ought. None must. Few do.* In any case, I suggest that between two people and between God and the soul, confession and forgiveness are important to put into words. I may have wronged you, and without any confession, you may realize I know and regret this, and I may know you forgive me. But there is still a point of setting things right by my telling you I am sorry and your telling me that you forgive me. I suggest that prayer can be like that.

Another obstacle to prayer involves believing God to be unsurpassably good. If God is supremely good and loving, what is the point of making requests of God? Does an omniscient, maximally good being need our advice or recommendations?

This is also a good objection. The very idea of advising God seems outlandish. But if there is to be a relational link between a person and God, it would seem very odd not to express one's deepest desires before God. If you long to see your friend cured of cancer, yes, God knows it, but it would seem, at least to me, unnatural to not express this in prayer. A prayer for healing and abundant other prayers with petitions (praying for victims of violence) or praise (gratitude for a birth, a wedding, gratitude for forgiveness) can provide a means for aligning ourselves with the goodness of God.

Some of our prayers may do more to change *us* (making us more compassionate, less self-centered) than they do to alter the outcome of events. Nevertheless, abundant biblical teachings (Matt 7:7–11) and narratives show God's action in response to prayer. Consider, for instance, cases of when Jesus heals in response to a plea, as in Matthew 8. Perhaps prayer can enter us into a kind of collaboration with the God of healing.

What is the point of repetition in prayer? Some Christian traditions of prayer involve numerous repetitions. For example, Orthodox Christians may repeat the Jesus Prayer a hundred times a day: "Lord, Jesus Christ, Son of God, have mercy on me, a sinner." This prayer is inspired, in part, by Matthew 20:29–34. Shouldn't saying it just once be enough?

Granted, sometimes repetition in prayer can become hollow or tedious. But it can also be a means of renewal and internalizing. I had a student who told me that once he says "I love you" to someone, he sees no point in merely repeating himself. "I'll let her know if I ever stop loving her," he said. Maybe that works for him and his beloved, but when I tell my beloved on Friday "I love you" and then on Saturday I say "I love you," it feels to me, and hopefully to her, that I am renewing my love for her. If you will forgive the analogy, when I kiss my beloved on Friday, I am not merely repeating the act when I kiss her on Saturday. Sure, kissing can become perfunctory and vapid, but I offer this testimony that *it can be and most often is delightful.*

On repeating the Jesus Prayer, the matter is more complex, for it is not like telling someone you love them a hundred times or akin to offering a hundred kisses. There are some texts on Orthodox prayer at the end of this book under references. Here I simply note that the repeating of the prayer can serve to quiet the mind of the one praying, in the course of centering oneself in what one takes to be the presence of God. Repetition is presented by some Orthodox saints as a means of coming closer to God.[10]

Consider the objection that the time spent in prayer might more effectively be spent in doing acts of compassion and fighting for justice. Some of us are frustrated when, after a mass shooting, politicians offer their "thoughts and prayers" but do nothing to support gun control or enact other measures to prevent such tragedies.

This objection has great force. One can too easily forgo one's moral, political, and spiritual duty to act justly. It seems gravely wrong when a felt duty to pray supersedes the obligation to act. Even so, prayer might open us up to a compelling experience of the divine that can energize our practical action. To fill out this suggestion, I cite Vaclav Havel's account of his transformative experience of love and harmony when he was a political prisoner.

Vaclav Havel (1936–2011) was a Czech statesman, dissident, poet, and playwright. He served as president of the Czech Republic from 1993 to 2003. He resisted Soviet Marxism and championed direct democracy. While he described himself as having an affinity for Christianity, he was not a professing Christian. All the same, I think that the following description of his experience resembles many descriptions of Christians and other religious believers who through prayer have a transforming vision of love that can lead to passionate, constructive, practical, political action. Havel wrote:

> Again, I call to mind that distant moment in [the prison at] Hermanice when on a hot, cloudless summer day, I sat on a pile of rusty iron and gazed into the crown of an enormous tree that stretched, with dignified repose, up and over all the fences, wires, bars and watchtowers that separated me from it. As I watched the imperceptible trembling of its leaves against an endless sky, I was overcome by a sensation that is difficult to describe: all at once, I seemed to rise above all the coordinates of my momentary existence in the world into a kind of state outside time in which all the beautiful things I had ever seen and experienced existed in a total "co-present"; I felt a sense of reconciliation, indeed of an almost gentle consent to the inevitable course of things as revealed to me now, and this combined with a carefree determination to face what had to be faced. A profound amazement at the sovereignty of Being became a dizzying sensation of tumbling endlessly into the abyss of its mystery; an unbounded joy at being alive, at having been given the chance to live through all I have lived

through, and at the fact that everything has a deep and obvious meaning—this joy formed a strange alliance in me with a vague horror at the inapprehensibility and unattainability of everything I was so close to in that moment, standing at the very "edge of the finite"; I was flooded with a sense of ultimate happiness and harmony with the world and with myself, with that moment, with all the moments I could call up, and with everything invisible that lies behind it and has meaning. I would even say that I was somehow "struck by love," though I don't know precisely for whom or what.[11]

Such a vision of being "struck by love" is widely represented in the mystical traditions of Christianity, Judaism, Islam, theistic Hinduism, and in other devotions to the divine. (See references at the end of the book.) Havel's extraordinary experience (whether prayer, contemplation, or meditation) is an example of how a transporting love and desire in response to the sacred can form part of a life of courageous action. It is evidence that there should be no divide between prayer or mysticism and action.

Prayer and other religious practices, such as the Eucharist (also called the Mass or Holy Communion), can be thought of as modes (portals, windows, or doors) to encountering the divine or sacred, rather than as objects of attention themselves. So, for many Christians, prayer and the Bible are the portals through which God is encountered. There is a profound difference between worshiping God and worshiping a religion. As the nineteenth-century Scottish theologian Thomas Erskine of Linlathen observed: "Those who make religion their god will not have a God for their religion."[12]

A last observation: prayerful meditation has been described by many spiritual directors as taking place in the present moment, as implied by the title of the eighteenth-century classic *The Sacrament of the Present Moment*, by Jean-Pierre de Caussade. Being focused on the present is not easy, as the famous neurologist and author Oliver Sacks wrote to a friend: "How often we have travelled, Mel! Always fleeing, always seeking, always deceiving ourselves, never arriving. Anchored to the Past, dreaming of the Future, and—in some fatal, blind sense—oblivious to the Present."[13]

Prayerful meditation may draw on the past, as we find in St. Augustine's spiritual use of memory (and in the passage by Havel), but this may be seen as summoning to the present moment our recollections (re-collecting ourselves, as it were), rather than escaping the present to dwell in a remote past. For a famous, humble account of retaining a continual state of living in the presence of God (*Coram Deo*), see the seventeenth-century work *The Practice of the Presence of God*, in which the friar Brother Lawrence recounts being in conversation with God in all his endeavors, whether it be in formal prayer or cooking or traveling to Burgundy to purchase wine for his monastery.

Chapter 8
Somersaults on the Grass

When tired, I sometimes misread signs and texts. Three brief examples: Upon arriving in Manchester, England, jet-lagged, I was startled to see a Barking Centre. I thought that this was delightful; what better way to calm down an urban population than to have a site where people could bark? I was disappointed when a second glance revealed that what I saw was actually a Banking Centre. This afternoon when I was doing some reading on trauma, I thought the author referred to a catastrophic harm as "highly successful," but a closer look revealed the text said "highly stressful." Third, this winter in an Arizona ER, I thought I saw the signage "How to strangle your patients," whereas it was actually a notice on transferring patients: "How to straddle your patients." Perhaps that misreading discloses a dubious pathology on my part, or perhaps it can be accounted for by the book I was reading then, a Brother Cadfael mystery in which there is murder by strangulation.

The three subjects in my examples of misreading (stress, trauma, and care for patients) concern an almost lifelong fascination with the process of recovery from trauma, especially the role of resilience. One of the most substantial traumas for most of my friends and family in the past few decades was the terrorist attacks on 9/11. Being a native New Yorker, I knew one person killed, but my family and friends knew hundreds. A cousin of mine was scheduled that day for a meeting in the Twin Towers; thankfully he missed it. How amazing that so many people, including Minnesotans from my adopted state, went to NYC to provide aid. The bravery and resilience of aid workers was awesome, including the action of a security officer who shielded those in his charge with his own body. More than twenty years later, that man, now an Episcopal priest here in Minnesota, is my spiritual confessor. Having saved people physically on that tragic day, I surmised he was well-positioned to help rescue me from my own faults and hear my contrition.

The use of therapy dogs with victims of trauma is well-documented. For almost nine years, my wife and I have been living with a Sheltie called Pip, who is a kind of freelance therapist. He almost never fails to raise smiles, and seems to instill hope and resilience among nearly everyone he meets. Pip does what we call "Pip-flips" by breaking into a run and then doing a somersault, winding up on his back, tongue out and smiling. No kidding. He has stopped cars as motorists break out with laughter or applause.

When Pip flips, he is inviting us to play. Although Pip has a birthmark on his nose in the shape of a cross and attends church with us, I can't swear he is a self-aware Christian. Still, his yen for play seems related to the spirit of Psalm 149:3. "Let them praise his name with dancing and make music to him with timbrel and harp." Well, Pip is not playing any timbrel and harp, but he does seem to entice us to dance. Actually, the invitation to dance comports very well with Dante's fourteenth-century masterpiece *The Divine Comedy*. In paradise twelve saints are dancing around Dante and Beatrice. Among the twelve are some of my all-time favorite saints: Anselm, John Chrysostom, and Hugh of St. Victor. They are dancing "with sublime festivity."

Perhaps you know W. H. Auden's poem "Funeral Blues," read beautifully in the 1994 film *Four Weddings and a Funeral*. In the face of trauma, many of us can relate to the poem's lament upon the death of a loved one. The poem begins: "Stop all the clocks, cut off the telephone, / Prevent the dog from barking with a juicy bone." And it ends without consolation.[14]

I have felt that despair many times; certainly upon the death of family and friends and, perhaps less dramatically but profoundly, at the end of a relationship. As a practicing Christian, Auden knew Christian convictions do not seal us off from deep, agonizing sorrow.

I would add, as many Christians have proposed, that if there is truly a good, loving God, inconsolable sorrow need not be the last word. Beyond "Funeral Blues," someday, after a long grief has been observed, it will once again be worthwhile to enjoy watching Pip doing somersaults.

There is a telling passage by G. K. Chesterton at the end of his book *Orthodoxy* (1908), which suggests a vision of what may lie on the other side of death and trauma:

> And as I close this chaotic volume I open again the strange small book from which all Christianity came; and I am again haunted by a kind of confirmation. The tremendous figure which fills the Gospels towers in this respect, as in every other, above all the thinkers who ever thought themselves tall. His pathos was natural, almost casual. The Stoics, ancient and modern, were proud of concealing their tears. He never concealed His tears; He showed them plainly on His open face at any daily sight, such as the far sight of His native city. Yet He concealed something. Solemn supermen and imperial diplomatists are proud of restraining their anger. He never restrained His anger. He flung furniture down the front steps of the Temple, and asked men how they expected to escape the damnation of Hell. Yet He restrained something. I say it with reverence; there was in that shattering personality a thread that must be called shyness. There was something that He hid from all men when He went up a mountain to pray. There was something that He covered constantly by abrupt silence or impetuous isolation. There was some one thing that was too great for God to show us when He

walked upon our earth; and I have sometimes fancied that it was His mirth. [15]

Not always, but there are times when I am playing with Pip, enjoying his exuberant somersaults, that I share such a fancy.

Part Two: **The Ox**

Chapter 9
The Ox and the Ass

The ox appears frequently in the Bible; it was an animal used for labor, and so it came to represent service, patience, strength, and humility. The ox, like the lamb, was also used as an animal sacrifice to God. In Luke's Gospel, the ox and the ass are linked when Jesus defends his healing on the Sabbath: "Doesn't each of you on the Sabbath untie your ox or donkey and lead it out to give it water?" (Luke 13:5; see also 14:5).

Luke and Matthew both offer narratives of the birth of Jesus. While neither Gospel mentions the presence of an ox and an ass, paintings of the nativity of Jesus often picture the animals reverently looking upon the holy family—for example, *The Portinari Altarpiece* (1475–78), by Hugo van der Goes. In the Bible, the ass was used as a work animal for carrying goods and people. In many paintings of the flight into Egypt, Mary is pictured riding on an ass. Jesus rides an ass or young donkey into Jerusalem (Luke 19:28–40). And yet the ass also frequently plays a comic role in literature, as in the ancient Roman satiric novel *The Golden Ass* and Shakespeare's *A Midsummer Night's Dream*. Arguably, the Old Testament story of Balaam's ass, who warns the prophet of danger, is comic (Num

22:21–38), or at least more comic than the only other talking animal in the Bible, the serpent in the Garden of Eden.

While I may be theologically skating on exceptionally thin ice, I suggest that the pairing of the ox and the ass in Christian art suggests that service, even to the point of sacrifice, can be fruitfully paired with humor. After all, St. Thomas More (d. 1535) was famed for his joking, even just before his martyrdom. It wasn't exactly a laugh out loud joke (he said something about needing help getting up on the scaffold where he would be beheaded, but not needing help getting down), though it did combine humor and his ultimate sacrifice for the sake of conscience. And we are told by Aslan himself in C. S. Lewis's *The Chronicles of Narnia*: "Laugh and fear not. . . . For jokes as well as justice came in with speech."[16]

It is on such grounds that I endeavor to offer college and university courses where there is some good-hearted laughter. For example, I encourage outlandish introductions for guest speakers. At St. Olaf College, many students are musicians and singers, and so they are eager to perform musical introductions to guest scholars. Probably the most dramatic was students carrying in a specialist in Daoism on a makeshift throne while they threw flower petals before him, singing a song of praise for his latest book. The visiting professor was speechless for at least a minute, being stunned by the performance.

Yes, there are also tears in and around my classes, for various reasons. In one advanced seminar of around twenty students, I think each student broke down crying during the semester; apparently, each one had been in a romantic relationship with another student and it had ended badly. Before one class a student asked: "Professor, would you mind if I used your office so I can cry before class?" Of course, I welcomed students to the office to cry whenever they wanted to. After all, in Tolkien's *The Return of the King*, Gandalf says, "I will not say: do not weep; for not all tears are evil."[17] Breaking campus rules, I also brought my playful Sheltie to school; he managed to raise smiles, even among the heartbroken. In a course in philosophy of religion, I sometimes invite a Hindu guru to lead us in a meditation with themes of compassion and joy.

One reason why a certain kind of laughter or entertainment can be helpful in addressing difficult topics (debating various rights and duties involving tough cases) is that in education we are called on to entertain—as in "contemplate" or "reflect on"—cases that we resist or find not just difficult but also painful. Calling into question deeply entrenched beliefs is not easy, and because this rarely involves comic moments, I encourage whatever good humor is on offer. Being able to laugh at oneself, for example, can be liberating. It has been speculated that one of Plato's tests that students had to pass to get into his academy was whether they could do philosophy while drinking wine. My test would require doing philosophy with a sense of humor.

I suggest that Luke's Gospel includes cases of what is called "observational comedy" in its many parables. Luke 15, for example, contains parables of the lost sheep, the lost coin, and the lost son. Observational comedy sees commonplace, everyday events in a new light, sometimes inviting an audience to identify with a character. Might you be a lost sheep or like a lost coin? Entertaining such possibilities seems humorous; I've only met one person who looked slightly like a sheep, and I've met no one who looks remotely like a coin. The lost son parable invites you to think of yourself as the prodigal son who leaves home and wastes his fortune, the parent who welcomes the son back, or the brother who resents the return of the son. It is comic insofar as it ends with a substantial, albeit not perfect, resolution.[18]

While endorsing a combination of the ox and the ass, I don't go quite as far as the sixteenth-century French essayist Montaigne on education. He seems to recommend a desperate measure if you have a student who is not interested in wise conversations or tales of voyages and bravery:

> If this pupil happens to be of such odd disposition that he would rather listen to some idle story than to the account of a fine voyage or a wise conversation when he hears one; if at the sound of the drum that calls the youthful ardor of his companions to arms, he turns aside to another that invites him to the tricks of jugglers; if by

PART TWO: THE OX

> his own preference, he does not find it more pleasant and sweet to return dusty and victorious from a combat than from tennis or a ball with the prize for that exercise, I see no other remedy than for his tutor to strangle him early, if there are no witnesses.[19]

Still, I wager that Montaigne was probably joking because he also adds one other alternative for handling the unresponsive student: "or apprentice him to a pastry cook in some good town."

Chapter 10
Lost and Found

A key declaration by Jesus in Luke's Gospel is that he "came to seek and save the lost" (19:10).

There are occasions when realizing that one is lost takes skill. Especially when your GPS is malfunctioning, you can be lost in a land, city, or building but not realize it. And one can be lost in a more peculiar manner, like the philosopher who claimed he is never lost because he always knows where he is: "I am always *here*," he would say, pointing to himself. "It's just that sometimes I don't know where everything else is." One can also imagine philosophers claiming to never lose track of time—they always know it is *now*—despite the fact that they have lost track of the time of day, as well as the day itself, month, and year. And while being lost in space and time can be disorienting, being lost personally (not knowing whether a relationship is good, being unclear about your actual desires or motives or values) can be terrifying.

Two dimensions of being lost and found are worth observing: both being lost and being found can take time and come in degrees. Just as losing or finding yourself may not be instantaneous, so it may be with God's searching. In a sense, you are never lost in the sight of an omniscient God, but finding you might be more like finding a friend or becoming a friend rather than finding your location in space and time. And becoming a friend—whether of a person, another creature, or the Creator—takes time.

One of the things that distinguishes Christian philosophers, as well as Jewish, Islamic, and Hindu theists, from many other thinkers is that we believe in a God who is seeking to have a relationship with us. That is why you find philosophers like St. Augustine and St. Anselm mixing their philosophical reasoning with prayer. To the ideals of other philosophies, prayer does not make much sense, because the God of Aristotle or Spinoza's God, for example, are not loving or mindful of creation. Believing that the God of Christianity is alive is something extraordinary. As C. S. Lewis observed:

> It is always shocking to meet life where we thought we were alone. "Look out!" we cry, "it's alive." And therefore this is the very point at which so many draw back—I would have done so myself if I could—and proceed no further with Christianity. An "impersonal God"—well and good. A subjective God of beauty, truth and goodness, inside our own heads—better still. A formless life force surging through us, a vast power which we can tap—best of all. But God Himself, alive, pulling at the other end of the cord, perhaps approaching at an infinite speed, the hunter, king, husband—that is quite another matter. There comes a moment when the children who have been playing at burglars hush suddenly: was that a real footstep in the hall? There comes a moment when people who have been dabbling in religion ("Man's search for God!") suddenly draw back. Supposing we really found Him? We never meant it to come to that! Worse still, supposing He had found us?[20]

The British poet W. H. Auden proposed that it was this Christian belief that God seeks us that makes God fascinating. "A god who is both self-sufficient and content to remain so could not interest us enough to raise the question of his existence."[21] As an aside, Auden also offered this warning: one reason to worry that your concept of God is not an authentic vision of the living God is if your "god" hates the same people you do.

The philosopher Charles Taylor notes how the relationship God seeks with us is sustaining, transforming. It is profoundly different from Taylor's story of how he might have this sudden relationship with Mont Tremblant:

> If I am a traveler from abroad and I ask where Mont Tremblant is, you don't help me by taking me blindfolded up in a plane, then ripping the blindfold off and shouting "There it is!" as we overfly the wooded hill. I know now (if I trust you) that I'm at Mont Tremblant. But in a meaningful sense, I still don't know where I am because I can't place Tremblant in relation to other places in the known world.[22]

If Taylor is right, being found by the living God is to find or discover oneself in a lifelong, growing relationship. A relationship that can deepen, wherever you are and whatever the time.

Chapter 11

Speaking Historically

Luke's Gospel opens with an address to Theophilus (a name or title meaning "loved by God" or "friend of God"):

> Many have undertaken to draw up an account of the things that have been fulfilled among us, just as they were handed down to us by those who from the first were eyewitnesses and servants of the word. With this in mind, since I myself have carefully investigated everything from the beginning, I too decided to write an orderly account for you, most excellent Theophilus, so that you may know the certainty of the things you have been taught.

Some scholars frown over the historical reliability of Luke and the rest of the New Testament. This is not exactly shocking, given the stories of angels and demons, miracles and prophesies, the resurrection of Jesus, and more. In my view, the judgments of historians often reflect their philosophical presuppositions. If you are not open to the possibility that there is a God of love who would be revealed in human history, the Bible as history is dead on arrival. And yet, it is hard to deny that if there is even a remote possibility of truth in its pages, then matters are profoundly intriguing and perhaps of incalculable importance.

One factor that does not irritate me (as someone who has written a history, not about the ancient world but about modern philosophy) is the lack of precise dating of biblical events. We are informed of events taking place when so-and-so was the emperor or governor or high priest and we are told the day of the week when some events occurred. That seems enough for me, because Luke and the New Testament seem more concerned with the meaning of events rather than precise chronology or calendar time. In some circles, the difference at issue is put in Greek: *chronos* refers to calendar time (quantitative measurement) whereas *kairos* refers to the meaning or significance (qualitative measurement) of an event. Yes, the Bible contains some chronology, but I read it as more attuned to meaning or *kairos*.[23]

For five years, I team-taught a course on war and peace (not the novel) with a professional historian. We definitely engaged in *chronos*, but the course was more about *kairos*. We looked at ancient, medieval, and modern histories of times of war and peace, but I think the most engaging classes involved interacting with guests who had firsthand experiences in war and peace: soldiers, diplomats, former prisoners of war, medical doctors on the front line. One friend of mine told us of his experience of being a sniper with the U.S. Army in the war in Vietnam. Apart from stories of bushcraft, reconnaissance, and tracking, he spoke in detail about the horror of killing. He spoke about obeying orders. His first order was to eliminate enemy soldiers using mortars to shell his camp; the soldiers he eliminated were four teenage girls. Also, he disobeyed orders, refusing to kill noncombatant civilians. Exact dates were not necessary for us to empathize; several students joined him in weeping.

When the focus is on meaning or *kairos*, you can sometimes see things you might miss otherwise. One international student from Eastern Europe told me that what was most moving about his experience in the war-and-peace class was a story of fatherhood and recovery. It was a story told by a veteran, who had been a sniper and clearly had PTSD. The veteran visited our class and told us that after the war he became a father. When five years old, his son asked him if they could go to see the fireworks that were scheduled at sunset. Maybe it was a July 4th celebration, maybe not. The date was not important. The man and his son, hand in hand, went to the fireworks display. The student called the father's act truly loving and brave. I learned later that the student had come from a family torn apart by Soviet oppression. Perhaps the veteran's story about being a father spoke to his own hope for healing in his family.

Luke's Gospel is not for the fainthearted. It includes a beheading and a crucifixion. The narratives unfold in a part of the world occupied by an imperial army. Jesus is born, grows up, and teaches in a dangerous world. Unfortunately, some of the dangers will seem all too familiar and real. But if you read the whole of it, I think you will find the *kairos* loving. There are stories of cowardice and fear, but in the end, they are outweighed by stories of overwhelming love and courage.

Chapter 12
Friendship for All Seasons

In the first chapter of Luke's Gospel, Mary and Elizabeth greet each other with joy. Mary is pregnant with Jesus, and Elizabeth is pregnant with John the Baptist. The scene is one of blessing and song. I suggest it is a wonderful portrait of friendship.

Friendships are celebrated in different biblical texts, especially in Proverbs (27:9), and in the narratives of friendships between Jonathan and David (1 Sam 20), Ruth and Naomi (book of Ruth), Elisha and Elijah (2 Kgs 2), even Jesus and John (John 13:23). The early centuries of the church fostered opposite-gender, non-romantic friendships, in contrast to ancient Rome where friendships were largely gender-exclusive.[24] Males had male friends; females had female friends. Early Christians, however, were encouraged to greet each other with a kiss of love (1 Pet 5:14); there was no admonition that the kissing only occur between people of the same gender or age or race or status, whether one was a soldier or merchant, parent or childless, slave or free. Of course, this was not a call for intimate sexuality, any more than the Eucharist was a call for cannibalism. Still, a kiss of love is a kiss of love.

Christian pictures of male-female friendships are beautifully portrayed in Boethius's depiction of his relationship with Lady

Philosophy in the sixth century and Dante's depiction of friendship with Beatrice in the fourteenth century. St. Bernard of Clairvaux's homilies on the Song of Songs suggest that marriage was understood to involve *eros* and romantic friendship; marriage was not principally about power, property, and lineage. According to Colin Morris's classic study *The Discovery of the Individual*, between the eleventh century and the fourteenth century, there was a profound shift to treasuring intimate, loving vulnerability between friends.[25] This had an impact in Christian art in the fifteenth and sixteenth centuries when, in Italian painting, saints were depicted in sacred conversation (*sacra conversazione*) with one another.

Perhaps the most historically important Christian work on friendship is *Spiritual Friendship (De Spiritali Amicitia)*, by Aelred of Rievaulx, a twelfth-century Cistercian monk who wrote about the beauty and conduct of friendship. One of his texts is Proverbs 17:17: "He that is a friend loves at all times."[26] Aelred was aware of human weakness, inconsistencies, and our feckless pursuits, but he maintained that if a mutual relationship falters, a true friend will never withdraw love even when that love is unrequited. In contemporary terms, I believe Aelred thought that while relationships were conditional (there is no duty to remain in an abusive "friendship"), love ideally should be unconditional.

A group of friends and I started a Saint Aelred Society in the late 1970s. Being a devotee of St. Aelred, I got into some trouble at a Harvard University conference on the meaning of life when I proposed that unrequited love was the highest form of love. I claimed it is an awesome, powerful love when you continue loving a friend even after your friend has betrayed the friendship. A world-famous psychologist objected that people who suffer from unrequited love are often subject to depression and grief. I had to concede that under those conditions, a person should probably forego continuing to love the former friend. But I made a partial defense of my original claim: I observed that people who are courageous probably don't live as long as cowards, and yet we still think that being courageous is a virtue and cowardice is a vice. Perhaps there are cases when unrequited love should be avoided,

I said, but maybe there are times when it's courageous and inspiring. I probably did not convince anyone, though one scholar at the conference appeared to nod in agreement; he was a follower of Kierkegaard, a philosopher who praised unrequited love. Kierkegaard thought that unrequited love displays the great power of love as unconditional and not dependent on reciprocity.

Luke's portrait of Mary and Elizabeth greeting each other reminds me of the stunning description of two ladies meeting in the fourteenth-century allegorical narrative *Piers the Plowman*, by William Langland. The poet describes himself as descending "into the depths of the earth" after hearing of the death and resurrection of Jesus. Here is his depiction about how the work of Christ reconciles Mercy and Truth; consider this exchange before the gates of hell:

> I drew back in the darkness and went down into the depths of the earth. And there, in accordance with Scripture, I dreamt that I saw a maiden, come walking from the west, and looking toward hell. Mercy was her name, and she seemed a very gentle lady, courteous and kind in all she said. And then I saw her sister come walking quietly out of the East, and gazing intently westwards. She was very fair, and her name was Truth; for she possessed a heavenly power that made her fearless.
>
> When these ladies, Mercy and Truth, met together, they asked each other about the great wonder that had come to pass—the noise and darkness and the sudden dawn. Why this light and radiance before the gates of hell?
>
> "The whole thing amazes me," said Truth; "I am now on my way to find out what it all means."
>
> "Do not be surprised," said Mercy, "for these are signs of great joy."[27]

The meeting of Mary and Elizabeth is depicted as joyful. Although we are not told this in the text, I like to think that when they met they shared a kiss of love, a harbinger of the love that will ultimately triumph, as we can see in Langland's vision of the sacred exchange between Mercy and Truth.

Chapter 13
Table Manners

Luke portrays Jesus at table. There is a banquet at the home of Levi (Luke 5), dinner at the home of a Pharisee (7), breaking bread in Bethsaida (9), hospitality at the home of Martha (10), a second dinner at a Pharisee's home (11), a third dinner with a Pharisee (14), hospitality at the home of Zacchaeus (19), the Last Supper (22), a meal at Emmaus (24), and a meal with the disciples (24). In fact, in Luke's Gospel and elsewhere in the Bible, one can find a guide for dining: be generous; don't seek the best seat; be humble; don't just invite prosperous people and your friends.

In the ancient world around the Mediterranean, hospitality (in Greek, *xenia*) was of great significance. In Homer's *Iliad*, two warriors cease fighting when they realize they had earlier been in a guest-host relationship. Violations of the guest-host relationship were considered vile and shameful. Prohibitions on harming guests were vital as one is profoundly vulnerable when receiving food from others (as we see in chapter 1 of Herodotus's *Histories* involving a profane, vengeful meal). And it is hard to avoid hospitality in the ancient world or today without reflecting on the rites and ethics of giving and receiving gifts.

Some philosophers have worried about the ethics of gifting. By making a gift to someone, you may place them under an unwelcome obligation of gratitude. And there seem to be some obvious rules about appropriate gifting. As a professor, it would not be fitting for me to bestow loaves and fishes, let alone bread and wine, among my students. And I have only once accepted the gift of a case of wine from the parents of a student, and that was after grades were in and graduation over. But Jesus seems to work outside many of the rules.

In Luke, Jesus appears to present himself, his teachings, healing, and food with almost reckless abandonment. He miraculously feeds more than five thousand people with loaves and fishes (9:13–17). He describes the kingdom of heaven as the ultimate, cosmic hosting: the heavenly banquet will be wide open with invitations (14:15–24). In the parable of the rich man and Lazarus, the rich man feasts daily and neglects poor Lazarus. His lack of generosity dooms the rich man (16:19–31). In Jesus' parable of the lost son, the errant son is welcomed back to his father's home without scolding or recrimination, but with a brilliant display of a lavish feast.

> But the father said to his servants, "Quick! Bring the best robe and put it on him. Put a ring on his finger and sandals on his feet. Bring the fattened calf and kill it. Let's have a feast and celebrate. For this son of mine was dead and is alive again; he was lost and is found." So they began to celebrate. (Luke 15:22–24)

The biblical scholar and Anglican bishop N. T. Wright observes the centrality of generosity in Christianity: "The great story of Scripture, from creation and covenant right on through to the New Jerusalem, is constantly about God's overflowing, generous creative love."[28] Such generosity is also made especially evident in Luke's stories of Jesus at table, his providing bounteous food, and his vision of a consummate, heavenly banquet.

Perhaps because of Jesus' teaching about the glory of a heavenly banquet, the early church held what became known as love feasts, or agape meals, to strengthen the communal bond among believers. This practice was criticized for being opulent. In the second century, Tertullian observed: "You attack our humble meals on the grounds that they are extravagant." In his work *Apology*, written in 197 CE, he offers this defense:

> The purpose of our meal is shown by its name: it is called by a word which to the Greeks means love [*agape*]. However much it may cost, it is gain to incur expense in the name of piety, since by this refreshment we comfort the needy.... Enough is eaten to satisfy hunger, and as much is drunk as befits the chaste.[29]

I love Tertullian's setting to one side the cost of such feasting, for that aligns the meal with an exchange between friends. St. Ambrose, in the fourth century, describes friendship: "Friendship is not a tribute, but a thing full of beauty, full of grace. It is a virtue, not a trade, because it is bought with love, not money, because it is acquired by competition in generosity, not by a haggling over its prices."[30]

Chapter 14
The Temple

The Jerusalem temple during Jesus' lifetime was the central focus of religious life. It was one-and-a-half-million square feet, roughly one-sixth the size of the city, and constructed with massive stones. Luke's Gospel narrates Jesus being presented at the temple as a child (2:22–39). He learns from scholars at the temple (2:41–52). Jesus spends time in the temple (22:53; see also 20:45—21:4). He cleanses the temple of merchants (19:45–47). Jesus also foretells the destruction of the temple (21:5–19). This is not a mere foretelling, but a sorrowful lament over immanent warfare, persecution, betrayal, and strife, as well as a prophecy that, over time and after the desolation, redemption will draw near (21:28).

The temple was destroyed in 70 CE by the Roman army under Titus, with thousands killed or enslaved. From a Christian point of view, Christ's death and resurrection provides redemption, but we still await an ultimate redemption when the times of war and destruction cease.

The significance of the temples in Jerusalem (the first built by King Solomon, the second by Herod the Great) for Jews, Christians, and Muslims is, of course, too complex and agonizing to address in a short essay. I focus, instead, on thinking about building a temple spiritually. I'm sure this sounds at first baffling and perhaps even irreverent, but consider texts like *The Interior Castle* by St. Teresa of Ávila, in which the contemplative soul is pictured as a castle with seven mansions. Inspired by that revered sixteenth-century Spanish mystic, I propose that some spiritual practices may be pictured as building an interior temple.

I suggest that intentionally setting aside time for prayer and meditation may fruitfully be visualized as building a visual site or imaginary space like a temple. The Jerusalem temple in Jesus' day was principally used for teaching and instruction, sacrifice, and worship. Imagining that during prayer you are entering a site dedicated to being in the presence of God (*Coram Deo*) can, in my experience, help sustain and structure meditation and focus. While this practice is new to me, such a visual exercise was employed not only by St. Teresa, but also by St. John of the Cross, St. Ignatius of Loyola, and a host of other spiritual directors and Christian poets (think of T. S. Eliot's "Little Gidding").

Of course, the physical destruction of the Jerusalem temple in 70 CE did not prevent Jews and Christians from finding new ways for worshiping and performing other religious rites in synagogues and churches throughout the world, albeit sometimes under conditions of horrific, catastrophic persecution. And we do well to recall times when sacred Muslim sites, mosques, and shrines have been savagely destroyed, as in the Siege of Baghdad in 1258 by a Mongol army. Still, in the midst of such ghastly brutality, I suggest that there is some consolation in the use of the interior imagination to sustain our devotion to a God more powerful than a Roman imperial or Mongol army, a God who calls us to overcome evil with good.

The practice of spiritually internalizing a temple dedicated to God's presence ties in with a key teaching of Jesus in the Gospel of Luke: "The kingdom of God is within you" (17:21).

If you decide to give this practice a try, I commend this verse from Habakkuk: "The LORD is in his holy temple. Let all the earth be silent before him" (2:20). Evelyn Underhill, Anglican spiritual director and author of the classic book *Mysticism*, says that "in the prayer of silence . . . the soul feeds upon God, draws new vitality from the source of all life."[31]

Another helpful point Underhill makes is that time and coherence are important. In 1937 she wrote: "We cannot begin the day by a real act of communion with the Author of peace and Lover of concord, and then go on to read a bloodthirsty newspaper at breakfast."[32] In today's terms, she would say: Don't transition too quickly from deep, prayerful meditation to social media.

Chapter 15

Traveling

The Gospels narrate Jesus' many travels or journeys, encompassing Bethlehem, Jerusalem, Egypt, Galilee, Capernaum, Nazareth, the Judean Desert, the River Jordan, Ephraim, Syrian-Phoenicia, Sidon, Bethany. He is in the countryside, cities, wilderness, on a hill or mountain. Including the supernatural itinerary, Christianity refers to Jesus walking on water, descending into hell after the crucifixion, and, after the resurrection, ascending into heaven. Speculation from time to time has included Jesus visiting Britain and India. In all the narratives of Jesus' travels, there is no mention of him or his disciples using maps, even though maps have existed for thousands of years (since the fourteenth century BCE in the ancient Near East). Perhaps knowledge of their environs, including roads, was so common there was no need to consult a map. In an extended type of cartography, the Gospel narratives can function as spiritual maps for us, guiding our thoughts and reflections on the teaching and events in the life of Christ.

Christian art and literature has often depicted the spiritual life in terms of travel: a journey, pilgrimage, or quest. Dante's *The Divine Comedy* and John Bunyan's *The Pilgrim's Progress* are two classics.

I suggest there are at least four important elements in the Christian portrayal of travel.

First, the travel narratives suggest that the spiritual life is not sedentary. It is a journey not just from place to place, but also over time. As such, different virtues may be needed at different stages.

Second, though this point may be rather tenuous, the stories of travels with Jesus seem to be unencumbered or, in a phrase, Jesus seemed to travel light. I can't find any references to Jesus having luggage. When we travel spiritually, perhaps we should minimize carrying dodgy baggage. When Jesus sends his disciples out on mission, he tells them: "Take nothing for the journey, neither a staff, nor a bag, nor bread, nor money" (Luke 9:3).

Third, Luke depicts Jesus often traveling with people ("Now large crowds were travelling with Jesus" 14:25). Perhaps Jesus' example should incline us to travel with a companion. A friend tells me of a sermon that included a question to the congregation: What is the best way to travel from Minneapolis to Chicago? Everyone spoke about different highways. After a bit, the pastor repeated the question and offered an answer. What is the best way to travel from Minneapolis to Chicago? *With a friend.*

Fourth, G. K. Chesterton suggested that we think of travel spiritually as following a path to what might be called home, a place of merriment and joy. He finds this theme in the work of Charles Dickens, whom he greatly honored. Chesterton wrote:

> But we have a long way to travel before we get back to what Dickens meant: and the passage is along a rambling English road, a twisting road such as Mr. Pickwick travelled. But this at least is part of what he meant: that comradeship and serious joy are not interludes in our travel; but that rather our travels are interludes in comradeship and joy, which through God shall endure forever. The inn does not point to the road; the road points to the inn. And all roads point at last to an ultimate inn, where we shall meet Dickens and all his characters: and when we drink again it shall be from the great flagons in the tavern at the end of the world.[33]

PART TWO: THE OX

Chesterton's vision of our travel suggests to me that, whatever adventures we have in our travels, the adventure includes an arrival in which we share our tales. Chesterton's picture of our arrival suggests a fifth element, drinking a fine ale together, but I will pursue that topic on another occasion. Perhaps we might discuss it when we reach the tavern at the end of the world.

I add just one more traveling tip—perhaps better described as a warning. In the early 1990s when I did some extensive cross-country driving in the United States, I brought along a crucifix. It was twenty-four inches long and called a passion or realistic crucifix (sometimes referred to as "bloody" for its graphic depiction of Christ's suffering). When cars or trucks came recklessly too close to my car, I would reach out with my left hand and wave the crucifix to ward off menacing vehicles. I hastily add that I did not do this as a prank or out of impiety; I regularly prayed with that crucifix. To my surprise, the crucifix-waving worked on numerous occasions; drivers seemed to react with horror, or perhaps mere puzzlement, and steered clear of me. Thus, in my view, I avoided many accidents. But some thirty years later, I do not recommend this strategy. Doing anything like that today might provoke road rage or some kind of distracting, dangerous escalation of emotion. I recommend instead saying (with or without a crucifix) one of the traveler's prayers noted under references at the end of this book.[34]

Chapter 16
Disciples

In Luke's Gospel, Jesus calls his first disciples by the Sea of Galilee (Luke 5). Jesus, as the great teacher, takes the initiative, calling people to follow him.

In my experience in education, I have known teachers who seek to perpetuate a subordination in the teacher-student relationship. Maybe this is tempting because, after all, the reason students seek out teachers is because they want to learn from them. But notice what Jesus says in Luke 6:40: "A disciple is not above his teacher, but everyone when he is fully trained will be like his teacher." This sounds like Jesus seeks disciples who will become peers. Perhaps the language of peer-ship is not quite right. After all, according to traditional Christianity, it is Jesus who redeems the world, not his disciples (neither the original disciples nor future followers or disciples of Jesus). All the same, Luke 6:40 may suggest Jesus as seeking companions. The term *companion* etymologically suggests one who shares bread with others (derived from the Latin *com* meaning "with" and *panis* meaning "bread or food"), and Luke and the other Gospels definitely describe Jesus sharing bread with the disciples, as well as with huge crowds of people.

PART TWO: THE OX

Another Lukan verse that suggests that discipleship is a kind of companionship is when Jesus says that the followers of his heavenly father are his siblings (8:21). This hints at an abiding familiarity and intimacy. What can spoil a teacher-student relationship (and perhaps a family relationship and master-disciple relationship) is an unhealthy self-consciousness or self-involvement. I know of this sin firsthand as a professor.

A student once came to my office, crying. She told me she had a brain tumor. I wept. But my weeping was only good for a few seconds. The first tears were out of empathy (maybe even love), but after about two seconds, I became self-conscious and addressed myself in a second-person sort of way: "Wow. Look at you," I said to myself. "You are actually crying. You must be an amazing professor! Much better than Jones down the hall, the stupid prig." Almost at once, I realized I had committed a sin, a blend of vanity, contempt for a colleague, and, worse, failing to be totally focused on the student.

When I confessed this to a priest, he commented that in that seemingly innocent moment I committed five of the seven mortal or deadly sins, all of them except for gluttony and lust. (By the way, a good acronym to use to recall the seven deadly sins is PALESAG: standing for Pride, Anger, Lust, Envy, Sloth, Avarice, Gluttony.) Lest this essay turn too confessional (and thus another example of inappropriate self-preoccupation), I bring this story up to highlight the radical reverse, exemplary virtue: Jesus' total self-giving and consistent, authentic, life-affirming companionship.[35]

I end with the traditional evening prayer for Christ's companionship. But not without a slightly pedantic note. I prefer the term *companion* to *comrade*, even though the latter can be quite positive. The etymology of *comrade* is sharing a room (derived from the Latin *camera*, meaning chamber). But sharing a room can be quite impersonal. Think of Melville's line in *Moby Dick* about the sailor who thought he would rather share a room with a sober cannibal than with a drunk Christian. The term *companionship* signals more of an intimate sharing. From the *Book of Common Prayer*:

Stay with us Lord Christ for evening is at hand. Be our companion in the way. Kindle our hearts. That you may be known in the breaking of the bread and prayers.

Part Three: **The Lion**

Chapter 17
The Lion and the Lamb

St. Mark's Gospel begins with "A voice crying in the desert" (1:3). The one crying is John the Baptist who "appeared in the desert proclaiming a baptism of repentance for the forgiveness of sins" (1:4). Early Christians read Mark's Gospel itself as a lion who cries out about the coming of Jesus, whose strength and courage (two traditional attributes of the lion) will be victorious over sin and death. A male lion's roar can be heard for five miles, establishing his territory in a terrifying manner. But while the Bible records the lion as a dangerous, brutal power, lions are also deemed as subordinate to the sanctity of God, as when Daniel is unharmed when thrown into a lions' den by a Persian king (Dan 6:21–22).

The lion has sometimes been viewed negatively, thanks in part to an epistle from St. Peter: "Your adversary the devil prowls around like a roaring lion, seeking someone to devour" (1 Pet 5:8). But the more positive significance of the lion prevails in Christian tradition. After all, Jesus is presented as a descendent of the tribe of Judah, which is traditionally symbolized as a lion, inspired by the blessing "Judah is a lion's cub" (Gen 49:9). Medieval bestiaries likened Jesus to a lion when Jesus sometimes wanted his identity as the Messiah kept secret (Mark 8:29), as it was believed that lions

PART THREE: THE LION

erase their footprints with their tails. What has been called the Messianic secret was to delay the inevitable, ultimate confrontation with Roman imperial power. In Jesus' day, members of the Roman Empire not only obeyed the emperor, but they also worshiped him as God's son, *Divi filius*. The kingdom of God that Jesus proclaimed was the opposite of the Roman kingdom; the first was ruled by the love of peace and forgiveness, the second by a love of power and domination. Only by concealing his true identity for a short time could Jesus teach, heal, and minister to those who were receptive to God's kingdom.

For me, picturing God as a lion has long been fresh and natural, having been enchanted my whole life by C. S. Lewis's The Chronicles of Narnia, the seven fantasy novels published from 1950 to 1956, in which the lion Aslan is divine. Perhaps due to over-enthusiasm for Aslan, a few years ago I interpreted the cascade of lions in my life as a sign that I should write a book about Aslan. You might be inspired too if the symbol of your school is a lion, the church you attend has a winged lion above its door (the cathedral's patron is St. Mark), your study center at university features three lion sculptures. I taught a course on Venice, which is dedicated to St. Mark and thus represented as a lion. Despite my almost fanatical devotion to Aslan, I am reminded that in the book of Revelation, it is *the lamb* that opens the scroll, not the lion. Revelation 5:1–7 describes this vision:

> I saw that there was a scroll in the right hand of the one sitting on the throne. The scroll was written on the inside and the outside, and it was sealed with seven seals. I saw a strong angel announcing in a loud voice, "Does anybody deserve to open the scroll, to undo its seals?" And nobody in heaven or on the earth or under the earth could open the scroll or look at it. I burst into tears because it seemed that there was nobody who was worthy to open the scroll or look inside it. One of the elders, however, spoke to me. "Don't cry," he said. "Look! The lion from the tribe of Judah, the Root of David, has won the victory! He can open the scroll and its seven seals." Then I saw in the midst of the throne and of the four

living creatures, and in the midst of the elders, a lamb. It was standing there as though it had been slaughtered; it had seven horns and seven eyes, which are the seven spirits of God sent out into all the earth. The lamb came up and took the scroll from the right hand of the one who was sitting on the throne.

What does that mean? Is Jesus the lion or the lamb? Jesus is both. He is the lion with powerful strength and courage, and he is also the lamb who was slain and was raised from the dead. After all, as the sixteenth-century Spanish mystic Luis de León points out in *The Names of Christ*, Jesus has been addressed and experienced under many names and images: Jesus is the good shepherd, a mountain, a fountain, living water, milk, and many other things, including bread and wine.[36] In the book of Isaiah, we read that one day "the ferocious lion" and "the gentle lamb" will be reconciled (11:6–9).[37] Perhaps they are already reconciled in the person of Jesus Christ.

I have met persons who combine the lion and the lamb. David Clayton, a monk in the Anglican religious order the Society of St. John the Evangelist, had immense fortitude and no-nonsense spirituality as well as a gentle, interior life of devotion. When he attended our church suppers in Boston for wayward people no one was more effective in getting guests to disarm—as he collected knives and guns—nor more ready to hear confession and offer reconciliation.

A friend once asked Father Clayton if her confession should include all sins since her baptism. "No," he replied, "but you should confess to any murders and adultery."

My friend laughed, "Father, I haven't committed any murders."

"Perhaps so," the priest replied gently but seriously, "but if you have committed murder, you should confess it."

I believe that exchange put on display his power to be disarming (the lion) and attract with gentle, wise love (the lamb).

Combining the lion and the lamb is not just good theology, but it can also be quite convivial. These creatures have been paired in the name of an award-winning, vegetarian-friendly English

PART THREE: THE LION

pub, The Lion and Lamb pub in Canfield. I am happy to buy the first round next to the portraits of a lamb and a lion enjoying a cocktail in that lovely Essex village.

Chapter 18

Vocation, Actually

A friend who is a professor of economics offered a course with the title "Vocation Reality." She wanted to engage students in the real search for their vocation, rather than in merely seeking a job. The term *vocation*, derived from the Latin *vocacio* meaning "summons," has a religious use, referring to our responding to God's call for how we should live and work. In a secular context, finding or choosing a vocation involves pursuing work you find satisfying, fulfilling, meaningful, and perhaps even ethically or socially significant.

About twenty-five students signed up for her class. On the first day, the professor was dismayed that five students thought they had signed up for a class on vacation rentals. It is somewhat shocking to me that undergraduates today would be interested in the economics of vacation rentals, but it is not surprising that the concept and search for a vocation might be confusing.

Mark's Gospel wastes no time in describing Jesus' calling the disciples (1:16–20). In fact, the whole Gospel, the shortest of the four, moves along at an alarming speed. The word *immediately* occurs forty-one times, averaging over two-and-a-half times per chapter. Maybe the people Jesus called to follow him responded

PART THREE: THE LION

instantaneously; Jesus may have had awesome, almost irresistible charisma. (I suppose I may have experienced an almost instantaneous conversion when I fell in love with essays by G. K. Chesterton.) Or perhaps Mark has condensed the events he narrates, and it took time for those called to respond. In any case, I believe it takes time to realize one's vocation—understood either religiously or in a secular context. Philosopher Charles Taylor proposes that becoming oriented in life takes time:

> My sense of myself is of a being who is growing and becoming. In the very nature of things this cannot be instantaneous. It is not only that I need time and many incidents to sort out what is relatively fixed and stable in my character, temperament, and desires from what is variable and changing, though that is true. It is also that as a being who grows and becomes I can only know myself through the history of my maturations and regressions, overcomings and defeats. My self-understanding necessarily has temporal depth and narrative.[38]

It is plausible to think that even if the disciples responded straight away to Jesus' call, it took their whole lives to grow deeper and deeper in their spiritual relationship with God.

Discovering my own vocation as a graduate student and then professor took time. And it was not easy. While still a graduate student, I was hired to teach ethics courses at the University of Massachusetts. I thought my first class of thirty students went well, until I showed up for the second meeting and I found the classroom empty. No one had shown up for class. I went to the men's bathroom and started crying. Was I that bad? Was my five years in graduate school a waste of time? After about ten minutes, a familiar looking student entered and asked how I was doing. I asked whether any students were interested in my course. He replied yes, of course, and observed that class was not supposed to start for another forty minutes. He then asked: "Are you crying?"

I replied: "No, I am just having trouble with my contacts." There was just one problem: I don't wear contacts. I was supposed to teach an ethics class, and I lied.

In retrospect, I suspect the student knew I was trying to cover up a breakdown. The whole class turned out to be wilder than I could have imagined. One woman came dressed every day as a witch (blood-red lipstick, chains, pencil with a miniature skull on it); one student was arrested for breaking into a computer network at Harvard (Harvard later hired him to be part of their security team); one student was a police officer who shot someone stealing a car; and one student "body-checked" me into the blackboard after I gave him a B for his paper that he thought deserved an A. And yet I got something out of the experience that was priceless: I decided to dedicate the rest of my life to being the best professor I could be. The path forward has not always been smooth.

One of the joys of being a professor is in helping students find their vocation. No, I do not call students to become disciples. But I am keenly aware that Taylor is right that it takes time to grow in self-understanding and find one's vocation.

Perhaps Mark himself went through some serious ups and downs. There is some evidence that Mark accompanied Paul and Barnabas on a missionary journey (Acts 12:25; 13:5), but deserted them on the way to Perga (Acts 13:13). When Barnabas wanted to bring Mark with him and Paul on another journey, Paul refused. This led to Paul and Barnabas going separate ways. Fortunately, there is also evidence that Paul and Mark became reconciled (Col 4:10; Phlm 24; 2 Tim 4:11). Maybe it took time for Mark to fully respond and deepen his own calling.

Chapter 19

Losing One's Head

The most famous beheading in the Gospels is the martyrdom of John the Baptist by King Herod. After his daughter-in-law danced for him, King Herod promised her whatever she wished. Prompted by Queen Herodias, her mother, she requested that the head of John the Baptist be brought to her on a platter (Mark 6:14–29).

Beheading was not uncommon in the ancient world; it occurs, for example, in the Old Testament (2 Kgs 10:8). Apart from the end of John the Baptist, the most well-known biblical cases are Judith's beheading of the Assyrian Holofernes (captured in Caravaggio's gruesome painting in 1571), David's beheading of Goliath (1 Sam 17:51, 57), and the Philistine's cutting off the head of Saul (1 Sam 31:9). There is some evidence that St. Paul was decapitated, and in Christian history, the church honors those who met a similar end, including Cyprian, James the Great, Olivia of Palermo, St. Valentine, Thomas More, Thomas Dingley, and others. For years I tried (unsuccessfully) to get my college, St. Olaf, to honor the death of King Charles I, who was beheaded on January 30, 1649. After all, both St. Olaf and Charles were kings who were martyred. Perhaps the school chaplain thought I was joking because he knew

I loved the fourteenth-century Arthurian tale *Sir Gawain and the Green Knight*. In that story Sir Gawain beheads the Green Knight, but the Knight was not dismayed; he simply picked up his head and walked away to challenge Sir Gawain another day. There is actually a term for carrying one's own severed head: *cephalophor*, from the Greek for "head-carrier."

There are other legends akin to the case of the Green Knight. St. Denis, first bishop of Paris, was beheaded in 250. Unhappy with the site of his execution, he walked, carrying his head, to his preferred burial site just outside of Paris. But such "golden legends" cannot replace the very real cases of intense horror in martyrdom and the brave profession of faith. In the oldest account of martyrdom, *The Martyrdom of Polycarp* in the mid-second century, we find this passage:

> When the Proconsul urged him and said, "Take the oath [worship the Emperor] and I will release; revile Christ." Polycarp answered: "Eighty-six years I have served Him, and He has never done me wrong. How, then, should I be able to blaspheme my King who has saved me?"[39]

I imagine that facing such a terrifying end, or any case of martyrdom, might be slightly assuaged to the extent that one has an inner calm certainty of God's presence.

An earlier essay spoke of the practice of picturing one's inner life as a temple. Another image of the inner life is worth considering: an enclosed garden (*Hortus conclusus*, Latin for "enclosed garden").[40] Actually, the two images are compatible as the temple in Jerusalem was a veritable garden sanctuary. The image of the enclosed garden was inspired, in part, by a passage in the Song of Solomon: "A garden locked is my sister, my bride; a garden locked, a fountain sealed" (4:12). In iconography the garden often portrays Mary and the Christ child, surrounded by flowers and fruits (lilies, strawberries, cherries). The image gradually evolved into the courtly romance *Roman de la Rose*. I suggest that such an interior space in which to treasure the presence of God (*Coram Deo*) might function as a tropical storm room, sometimes called a safe room or a panic room, to keep one safe during times of fire, wind, rain,

PART THREE: THE LION

and other dangers. Christians killed for their faith seem to draw strength from an inner certainty and trust in God's presence. St. Ignatius of Antioch offered this prayer: "Allow me to be eaten by the beasts, which are my way of reaching God. I am God's wheat, and I am to be ground by the teeth of wild beasts, so that I may become the pure bread of Christ."[41] People don't say things like that without an awesome, inner certainty.

I can report that the use of the *Hortus conclusus* imagery can be of use in troubled times. I was surprised one day when a student (I'll call Arthur) asked if he could adopt me as his grandfather. His grandfather had just died, and he needed me to fill that role. I agreed. Late in the term, Arthur removed a portrait of Chaucer from our classroom in order to make a point about "the aesthetics of absence." Regardless of the academic merits of the removal, somehow campus security descended on the class and treated Arthur as though he were a criminal. The painting was recovered and I defended my new grandson. My defense took place in a small room with the dean of students screaming at me. The confrontation was not like facing wild beasts or an executioner, but it was a scathing, calamitous attack on my integrity and professional standing.

Spiritually, I went to my *Hortus conclusus*. After an hour of listening to the dean's rage, I gently pushed back about Arthur's innocence and mistreatment. The dean wavered. In an odd transition, he said that I was loved by many on campus, but he was hated. I told him that was not true; if it appeared that some student disliked him, it was not personal. Some students may hate his disciplinary actions, I said, but that is not the same as hating him.

From a position of inner strength, I found myself saying something like the following: "I feel your anger, but ask me how I feel about you." He looked shocked. I think he expected me to use the kind of profanity he'd hurled at me.

"I feel about you, the same as I have always felt," I said. "I love you. *And I would trust you with my life.*"

The dean started crying. We embraced. And the next day, I gave him an expensive German pen as a peace offering.

My story cannot be compared with tales of John the Baptist, St. Paul, Polycarp, and others who were executed for their faith. But maybe my experience of retaining an inner, spiritual calm tapped into a source of strength that is available both in times of momentous violence wrought by imperial power, as well as in the comparably calmer context of academia when an adopted grandfather was called on to defend his grandson.

Chapter 20

Requests

In Mark's Gospel, chapter 10, verses 35–40, there is this exchange:

> Then James and John, the sons of Zebedee, came to him. "Teacher," they said, "we want you to do for us whatever we ask."
>
> "What do you want me to do for you?" he asked.
>
> They replied, "Let one of us sit at your right and the other at your left in your glory."
>
> "You don't know what you are asking," Jesus said. "Can you drink the cup I drink or be baptized with the baptism I am baptized with?"
>
> "We can," they answered.
>
> Jesus said to them, "You will drink the cup I drink and be baptized with the baptism I am baptized with, but to sit at my right or left is not for me to grant. These places belong to those for whom they have been prepared."

The exchange is haunting. The initial desire of these brothers that Jesus do *whatever* they ask seems haughty at first, but perhaps it was flattering. It suggests they see Jesus as powerful. And they don't ask for great wealth. Glory is on their minds, though the kind of glory Jesus offers is not the kind that radiates from an earthly throne room.

I am inclined to think there is something admirable about the request of these brothers. Sure, the bit about sitting on either side of Jesus in glory seems imperious and would suggest that they are superior to other followers of Jesus. But a desire to be near Jesus and to undergo or join him in his mysterious journey, symbolized by drinking from a cup and being baptized, might be read as amorous devotion.

My prayer life is sometimes a calming refuge, like entering a *Hortus conclusus*, or enclosed garden. I sometimes focus on a reproduction of 1410 painting *Virgin and Child in the Hortus Conclusus*. At other times my prayer life is frenzied with all kinds of requests. I ask God to heal this person, to save that marriage, to prevent this person from self-harm. Though requesting practically everything, so far, I have not asked to sit on a throne next to Jesus.[42]

In my experience, there are many dimensions to requests—to whom or what you are making the request, what is being requested, and then how the request is made. All three are on my mind when I make requests.

In my professional life, the most dramatic request I have ever made was to honor a colleague's expectation of her salary. I was chair of my department and faced a quandary: Jane was led to believe her salary was X, but the provost only offered a fraction of X. I practiced making a request of the provost, a large bearded man who, in my mind, looked like a huge bear. I knew he liked the word *redeem*.

I rehearsed making my request with my wife, Jil. I planned to get super close to the provost's face. I usually don't get that close, so I practiced doing it with Jil.

On the day of my request, I waited for the provost by the school mailboxes. I then pounced, sort of. I explained that Jane was a brilliant professor and she had received verbal assurance about her salary. "I believe she deserves that salary and this is a situation," I said, moving so close to the provost's face I almost touched his beard, "we need to redeem." I then lingered until he stepped back, maybe in shock. In any case, the provost said something like he agreed and he would see what he could do. Jane got the promised salary.

I wonder whether Jesus used such a technique when he made requests of his followers. Did he get super close on occasion? I also wonder whether Jesus smiled at James and John, knowing that one day in the Garden of Gethsemane Jesus would ask the Father to do something for him. He would ask to not drink from the cup set before him. "Take this cup from me. Yet not what I will, but what you will" (Mark 14:36). Perhaps when the Father's will was made known to Jesus, it was so compelling because of the unimaginable closeness of Jesus and the Father.

The brothers James and John survived Jesus' death and resurrection. I like to think that in the following years they experienced the awesome, intimate presence of the resurrected Jesus, for they faithfully witnessed to Jesus' redeeming love at great cost. According to Christian tradition, James was killed by Herod in the year 44, and while John lived to be a hundred years old in Ephesus, he suffered imprisonment for his faith on the island of Patmos. I imagine heaven is not a sedentary affair; and amid all its dynamic changes, perhaps the brothers are, on occasion, side by side with their Lord.

Chapter 21
Questions

My father used to tell me that the secret to being interesting is to ask questions. He probably had in mind dinner parties and other social occasions. In any case, if Dad was right, then Jesus in Mark's Gospel is supremely interesting. Jesus asks questions in 2:23–28; 3:1–6; 4:21–25; 4:40; 8:12, and more. Nine questions appear in 8:17–21. In the ancient world, probably only Socrates came close to asking so many questions. Socrates and Jesus had some things in common.

Both Socrates and Jesus loved wisdom. They called on their contemporaries to renounce injustice. They prized truth-telling and disdained hypocrisy and pretentious pride. Both urged people to care about their souls. Neither charged money for their teaching. Both of them had followers or disciples who would inspire a global movement (philosophy and Christianity). Both preferred speech to writing. In fact, neither of them wrote scrolls or books or epistles, but their followers did. Both of them were executed by the governing state after a trial; Socrates was executed by the Athenian democracy in 399 BCE and Jesus was crucified in the year 33 by imperial soldiers under the authority of the Roman governor Pontius Pilate.

Among the major differences in the lives of Socrates and Jesus, consider these two. In Plato's *Phaedo*, Socrates calmly accepts his death. For him, death involves the release of his soul from his body, which Socrates views as a great good. Life in the material world has its pleasures, but to be disembodied is akin to being released from a burden or prison. In contrast, Jesus dies in agony. He regards his bodily life as a great good, for after the mutilation and tortuous death, he rises from the dead as the resurrected bodily Jesus. As evidence of Jesus' love of bodily life, notice how many miracle stories involve the restoration of bodily integrity (bringing sight to the blind, healing the lame).

As a philosopher in the Socratic tradition, I share Socrates's affirmation that we are, or have, souls that are not identical with our bodies. But as a Christian, I am drawn to the affirmation of the goodness of embodied life. Too often, Christians have been accused of denigrating the body and of focusing too much on the soul. As I write this, a good friend is in the last stages of dying from cancer. When his body fails, I pray that his soul is in God's care. In the face of tremendous bodily injury, it is tempting to give the soul our primary focus, but we dare not lose sight that we are created in an embodied life, in which we live as unified beings with soul and mind integrated with our body.

A second difference between Socrates and Jesus concerns their mission or vocation. Socrates described himself as a gadfly, an annoying force seeking to arouse his contemporaries to love wisdom and care for their souls. While Socrates also spoke of his having an inner spiritual voice (in Greek, *daimon*), he never claimed to be sent from God or to perform miracles or forgive sins. (Probably Socrates accepted, at least ritually, the polytheism of his time.) But when Jesus asks the question "Who do you say that I am?" (Mark 8:29), he accepts this answer from Peter: "You are the Messiah." Christ is believed to be the one sent by the God of Israel to lead the people out of sin and death and into the kingdom of God.

Christians sometimes don't know quite what to think of Socrates. While, unlike Socrates, we wish to give greater praise to

God for our material embodiment, and we don't see Socrates as the Messiah, we are not comfortable seeing him in hell. This is why, in the *Divine Comedy*, Dante locates Socrates in limbo, along with some companionable chaps like Homer, Ovid, and Aristotle. I think the contemporary Christian philosopher Peter Kreeft improves on Dante. With wit and wisdom, he has written many books about when famous thinkers (Kant, Hume, Marx, Freud, and others) die and meet Socrates, who then questions them about their philosophical works.[43] Spoiler alert: Socrates does not succeed in turning his thinkers into Christians. He does what the historical Socrates did best: he so questions their certainty about life and death, that these great thinkers are humbled and at least become more open to the One who is greater than Socrates.

Chapter 22
Naked

One of the most puzzling passages in all the Gospels is this:

> And a certain young man was following him, clothed only in a linen cloth on his naked body. And they attempted to seize him, but he left behind the linen cloth and fled naked. (Mark 24:51–52)

The scene takes place in the Garden of Gethsemane where Jesus is betrayed and arrested.

There has been quite a bit of speculation on the man's identity. Jerome thought he was James, the brother of the Lord. John Chrysostom thought he was John the Apostle. Because the story only appears in Mark's Gospel, some have wondered whether it was Mark himself or a member of his household. A friend suggests that the man fleeing naked from the garden may have been a harbinger of an unstoppable event—crucifixion of naked Christ. In the early 1960s, a professor at Columbia University claimed to have found an account of a homoerotic narrative by Mark about Jesus teaching the secrets of the kingdom to a young, naked man, but it turned out to be a forgery.

I will put to one side various studies about Jesus' sexuality in Christian literature and art. Nor will I defend the historical reliability of this biblical story, but my inclination is to think it is true, both in light of the New Testament being divinely inspired and on the grounds that the scene is so bizarre there would seem to be no reason to include it unless some eyewitness had seen the young, naked man fleeing. I suppose the presence of someone naked in a garden might echo Genesis 2:25, when Adam and Eve are described as naked in the Garden of Eden, but that would be rather tenuous. Adam and Eve are not ashamed then, whereas the young, fleeing naked man is probably ashamed or frightened.

While it is difficult to ferret out a theology of nakedness from that short verse in Mark, it is good to note how some Christians historically have prized nakedness. There is some evidence that early Christian baptisms were done in the nude. In 1206 when Francis renounced his earthly family and its wealth, he took off all his clothes as he dedicated himself to his heavenly Father.[44] In the mid-seventeenth century, Quakers sometimes went naked as a sign of renouncing the world.

There is an old Christian precept: follow naked the naked Christ. Jerome embraced this precept metaphorically, and it was used later by Franciscans, the idea being that one should follow Christ without pretense or disguise, but in humility and poverty. The precept also can remind us that God sees us as we are.

In art history, there used to be a distinction between being naked and being nude. The second was used to refer to an aestheticized body, like Michelangelo's *David* or Botticelli's *Birth of Venus*, whereas being naked meant simply not wearing any clothes. Being naked before God is a matter of being before God not as some idealized character, but being in the presence of One who knows all our thoughts and desires, our secrets and aspirations, our disappointments, dreams, scars, blemishes, and injuries. And loves us. Moreover, God's love may be seen in the sacrifice of Christ. Being crucified naked was part of the humiliation of this form of Roman execution. All four Gospels agree: Jesus was stripped of all his clothes. This gives poignancy to the precept about our being naked following the naked Christ; *Nodus nudum Christum sequi*. Moreover, that precept lines up well with a famous verse from the book of Job: "Naked I came from my mother's womb, and naked I will depart. The LORD gave and the LORD has taken away" (Job 1:21). Actually, verse 21 does not end there. The last line says: "Blessed be the name of the LORD"!

Chapter 23
Relics

The veneration of relics—the bones or bodies of saints and other sacred objects—has not disappeared. Just last year almost a half million people completed the Pilgrimage of Compostela, where the Cathedral in Santiago houses a host of relics, including the body of St. James, the apostle. Of course, some of those pilgrims had other agendas/goals than venerating relics, but such pilgrimage sites have their roots in reliquaries.

The term for harvesting relics is *exhumation*. Relics are divided into three categories: the body or part of the body of a saint, a possession of a saint, and something that the saint touched. The story of some relics is curious. When St. Thomas Aquinas died, some Cistercian monks cut off his head and hid it from the Dominicans. The body of St. Mark was in Alexandria, Egypt, where he was martyred in the year 68, until 628 when two Venetian merchants translated it (when relics are moved, the term *translate* is often used) to Venice, hidden in a barrel of pork and vegetables. St. Mark became the patron saint of Venice; the city is symbolized by a winged lion.

The sites of relics are awesome. The Basilica di San Marco in Venice is stunning. The Romanesque church in Vézelay, France, housing a relic of Mary Magdalene is extraordinary. And who doesn't love Sainte-Chapelle, housing the crown of thorns in Paris?

I was put in charge of the safety of a relic on Good Friday 1982 at the Episcopal Monastery of St. John the Evangelist in Cambridge, Massachusetts. It was a small piece of wood believed to be part of the holy cross on which Jesus was crucified. At the beginning of that Good Friday, April 9, did I honestly believe the origin story to be true? It can be traced back to St. Helena's discovery of the cross in the early fourth century. That was good enough for me to think it is was possible. Besides, in some matters of life I have a "what if" policy. For example, when I was studying at the University of Rhode Island, a professor, who was teaching James Joyce's *Ulysses*, claimed to be the reincarnation of Joyce. I chose to take his course. I do not believe in reincarnation, but what if I'm wrong and the professor is James Joyce? (He had an uncanny familiarity with Dublin at the start of the twentieth century.)

Setting aside that professor, on that Good Friday, I was dressed in acolyte vestments and on the lookout for Roman Catholics who might try to steal the small piece of wood that might be a fragment of the holy cross. When it came time for me to venerate the relic, I changed my sensibility toward the spiritual aspect of material things.

Each of us in the monastery slowly approached the relic and made three full prostrations. Three times we stretched out on the marble floor of the chapel, arms reaching outward. When I kissed the relic with my lips, the reality of the life and death of Jesus became vividly and undoubtedly clear. It felt like falling in love. Or, after falling in love, the first romantic kiss. Decades later, I look back on that event as instilling in me a lifelong love of the Eucharist.

In that moment of veneration, I came to truly believe in the power of God to transform ordinary things like wood, bread, and wine into that which is so extraordinary that one can only approach with humble, outrageous, almost absurd self-abasement. I moved from a position of "what if" (what if she or he loves me) to a faithful affirmation (how good it is to love and to be loved). Perhaps it was akin to the transformation C. S. Lewis underwent when he transitioned from *Credere Deum est* (to believe God exists) to *Credere in Deum* (to believe in God) or, more specifically in my case on that Good Friday, to *venerandum Christi incarnatum* (revere the incarnate Christ). The event was far more wondrous and long-lasting in effect than if I'd actually studied under the reincarnation of that great Irishman Joyce, who authored the most important modernist novel, *Ulysses*, a story involving several Dubliners during one day in 1904. Occasionally, I honor Leopold Bloom Day, sometimes called Bloomsday, when that main character in *Ulysses* wandered through Dublin on June 16. But almost daily I honor the ongoing experience that flowed from the moment I venerated a relic on the second Friday in April, 1982, anno Domini.[45]

Chapter 24

Wild Beasts

In the first chapter of Mark's Gospel, we read "And He [Jesus] was in the wilderness forty days being tempted by Satan and He was with the wild beasts and the angels were ministering to Him" (1:13). The wilderness of ancient Israel had abundant wild beasts, including the Asiatic lion, gazelle, wild boar, Syrian brown bear, wolf, deer, wild ox, and hippopotamus. In general, we think of wild beasts as large, not tamed or domesticated four-footed animals. Mice, for example, are not large enough to be thought of as wild beasts (though they can be difficult to control).

Some saints have a good track record with wild beasts. The story of St. Francis of Assisi taming the wolf of Gubbio is a favorite. He talks with the wolf, and the wolf agrees to no longer terrorize the town people. The wolf is fed by the people and lives to a ripe old age. Still, wild beasts can be dangerous. The hymn "I Sing a Song of the Saints of God" contains these lines: "And one was a soldier, and one was a priest, and one was killed by a fierce wild beast." On rare occasions when I am feeling a little anti-clerical, I sing "and one was killed by a fierce wild priest."

What did Jesus do with the wild beasts? I am not opposed to all hunting, but I doubt Jesus hunted them. Maybe he played with some of them? Or perhaps Jesus was able to communicate with them. Not impossible. Possibly, Jesus followed Aristotle's advice about what to do when confronting a dangerous dog or other animal. He suggested sitting down, remaining calm, and addressing the beast on the same level. We simply don't know, but I like to think that Jesus not only resisted the temptations of Satan, but maybe with some angelic assistance, he also survived being with wild beasts for over a month.

From time to time, I have to be around fierce beasts in the form of dangerous, discordant professors and students. The students have not been as distressing as the professors have been. In a philosophy of mind class, one student had a habit of yelling at me. He also yelled at me during office hours and over Zoom. I endured his behavior until he turned on Alesha, a student who was going through a rough time because her brother, a Muslim, had been attacked in Chicago by an anti-Muslim gang. The yelling student declared he had no idea whether Alesha had any feelings and thoughts, but he was more sure that advanced computers did have some. All I had to do was calmly ask him to stop yelling and be more considerate. He apologized, and peace was (miraculously?) restored.

Professors have been more challenging. I attended a beastly conference at the University of Notre Dame, which brought together biblical theologians and Christian philosophers. Campus security was increased. (No joke, no hyperbole.) In one memorable moment a biblical theologian told a philosopher that if Jesus had heard his paper, Jesus would roll over in his grave. Evidently, the theologian did not accept the historicity of the accounts of Jesus' tomb being empty.

One beast, that is, one professor who was like a beast, challenged me publicly after I gave a paper on the soul. "Isn't your argument weak?" he asked me. "In fact, isn't the probative force of your argument zero?" He made this charge with such confidence and ferocity, I felt utterly down and out. Years later, with the help of a therapist, I realized that my emotional collapse was aided by the professor's age and his behavior that reminded me of a brother who relentlessly criticized me from childhood to early adulthood. The professor's accusation conjured up my nearly fratricidal sibling.

Despite my ghastly humiliation, my faith kept me from abandoning my thinking about the soul. I was defending a position on the soul long held by theologians I deeply admired, Origen, Augustine, Anselm. I came to feel that we might all be wrong, but this was not obvious and the professor's objections had not been decisive. Besides, I follow One who not only resisted the temptations of the dark lord (Satan), but who also lived for forty days among wild beasts. Perhaps Jesus himself had to face serious philosophical challenges from Satan and the beasts.

I stayed calm in my overt response to the professor and took refuge internally in my soul. After some therapy, I sat down and wrote a book defending my argument. Many years later, I saw the professor, who looked older and less dangerous. He told me he had read my recent work and agreed with me on all points. I felt that the former beast had become a ministering angel.[46] Thanks be to the God of all creation, wild and domestic, human and nonhuman. And forgive me, Lord, when I myself might act like a wild beast; help me not to yell and, instead, to be considerate of the well-being and vulnerability of those I encounter, including professors, students, and especially readers of this book.

Part Four: **The Eagle**

Chapter 25
Mystics in the Library

As I begin the fourth part of this tetramorphic set of essays, I cannot resist the language of aviation (my father was a pilot, starting with biplanes and graduating to jets). John's Gospel is likened to the eagle in its soaring language. This Gospel seems to take off from its opening verse: "In the beginning was the Word, and the Word was with God, and the Word was God."

In these eight essays, I continue to write in a Chestertonian spirit and do not engage with technical philosophy or biblical scholarship. The essay themes are inspired by themes from John's Gospel.

I studied the Gospel of John and the gnostic gospels under Professor George MacRae at Harvard Divinity School. Those were heady days in the 1970s as the world was still coming to terms with the Nag Hamadi library of gnostic texts, discovered in 1945. MacRae's colleague John Strugnell had been under fire as editor in chief of the Dead Sea Scroll library project for his slow and reluctant release of the scrolls to international scholars. The dissemination of the scrolls was speeding up. Students were invited to translate some of these ancient texts. Professor Margaret Miles was taking a fresh look at historic Christian authors, from Ignatius

PART FOUR: THE EAGLE

of Antioch to Thomas Aquinas, emphasizing the integration of soul and body spiritually. The fruit of that new look was *Fullness of Life* (now available through Cascade Books). Theological flying conditions seemed CAVU, or Ceiling And Visibility Unlimited, an aviation term for ideal flying conditions.

One thing emerged with great clarity in my study of John and gnosticism under MacRae: John's Gospel is not gnostic. Gnostics tended to denigrate the material world and deny the reality of the incarnation. They portrayed Jesus as a mystic sent by God (the true God who was not the same as the god who created the material world) to lead us out of this world to a heavenly, immaterial kingdom. John's Gospel affirms the reality of Jesus as incarnated. "The Word became flesh and dwelt among us" (1:14). Jesus eats, drinks, sleeps, and dies. John's account of the crucifixion includes a detail missing from other gospels: "But one of the soldiers pierced his side with a spear, and at once there came out blood and water" (19:34). Jesus seeks to repair bodily injury: he makes a lame person walk (5:1–18) and restores sight to the blind (9:1–41). He blesses a wedding with fine wine, thus affirming the goodness of sexual union (2:1–11), raises Lazarus from the dead (chapter 11), and feeds a multitude (6:1–15). John recognizes the darkness of the world (1:5), its sins and evil, and describes Jesus as overcoming such evil (16:33).

In the course of my studies, I came to appreciate the difference between Christian, Johannine mysticism (from the apostle John's teachings), and forms of mysticism that seem escapist and disembodied. I found a treasure trove of Christian mysticism in the divinity school library and began what would become decades of a mystic-a-month project. December was devoted to *The Cloud of Unknowing*, followed by Julian of Norwich in January, St. Catherine of Siena in February, and so on. As I write this essay in November 2024, the mystic this month is Thomas à Kempis.

The grounded form of Christian mysticism that I commend is captured in the title of Evelyn Underhill's book *Practical Mysticism*. It was published in England at a time of crisis: the outbreak of a world war in the summer of 1914. In the preface she writes:

> This little book, written in the last months of peace, goes to press in the first weeks of the great war. Many will feel that in such a time of conflict and horror, when only the most ignorant, disloyal, or apathetic can hope for quietness of mind, a book which deals with that which is called the "contemplative attitude to existence" is wholly out of place. So obvious, indeed, is this point of view, that I had at first thought of postponing its publication.[47]

She persisted with the book's publication on the grounds that in times of crisis and hardship, a practical mysticism is needed more than ever. Underhill wrote:

> Yet the title deliberately chosen for this book—that of "Practical" Mysticism—means nothing if the attitude and the discipline which it recommends be adapted to fair-weather alone: if the principles for which it stands break down when subjected to the pressure of events and cannot be reconciled with the sterner duties of the national life. To accept this position is to reduce mysticism to the status of a spiritual plaything. On the contrary, if the experiences on which it is based have indeed the transcendent value for humanity which the mystics claim for them—if they reveal a higher truth and greater reality than the world of concrete happenings in which we seem to be immersed—then that value is increased rather than lessened when confronted by the overwhelming disharmonies and sufferings of the present time.

In my ongoing encounter with John's Gospel and the mystic-a-month project, I found an integration of the mystical sense of the transcendent and a commitment to facing the concrete moral, political, and cultural turmoil of our time.

I end with a favorite phrase of Professor MacRae's. In the course of an hour of brilliant lecturing, the professor would look at his hands, chalk-covered from writing English and Greek terms on the blackboard, and say, "To be sure . . . ." To be sure, I believe that the Johannine integration that Underhill witnessed to is more important today than ever.

Chapter 26
Hell and How to Get There

In the Gospel of John, the term *hell* does not appear, but some passages imply that a failure to enter the kingdom of God can leave one in peril of punishment, condemnation, and darkness (John 3:3, 16–20). This fits the portrayal of hell in the other Gospels.

Within Christianity there is a significant tradition, often called universalism, according to which God will ultimately save all persons, revealing to all an overwhelming, irresistible love. Universalists include many of the great theologians, like Origen of Alexandria, Gregory of Nyssa, St. Isaac the Syrian, and, moving ahead many centuries, George MacDonald, and today Robin Parry, Alvin Kimel, Marilyn McCord Adams, Andrew Hronich, Thomas Talbott, and others.[48] Universalists sometimes believe there are cases of persons being separated from God's loving will, but they do not see this hell or hellish condition as everlasting punishment. They hold that, in the end, God's love will overcome our resistance to following God's omnipotent love. Christian universalists need to interpret biblical references that appear to depict hell as everlasting as admonitions (warnings about the gravity of sin) rather than literal predictions of endless torment. To some traditionalists, this may seem too liberal or unbiblical, but many Christians historically and today have adjusted their biblical interpretations in light of experience and reason. For example, some biblical texts seem to teach that the faithful will flourish and the wicked will not prosper in this life (Ps 1); these verses have been re-interpreted as aspirations (it would be good for the faithful to flourish; and we should aspire that it should be so) or as admonitions (the wicked should not prosper in this life), or as eschatology (the faithful will flourish and there will be a divine judgment against the wicked or wickedness in the next life). Another adjustment has been to modify early Christian expectations of the immanent return of Jesus (John 21:22) as instructing us to live in perpetual (or long-term) expectation of Jesus' second coming. Whether or not Christian universalism is biblical, I leave to others to sort out.

I hope the universalists are right, but in this essay let us consider how we try to create hell for ourselves and others or try to go there, even if such a hell is not everlasting. We can think of hell as a spatial place, a kind of domain, or a state of being, irrespective of location. I am inclined to think of hell as both a state of being in this world and beyond death. That hell can be here and now is one of the insights of Christopher Marlowe's sixteenth-century play *Dr. Faustus*. Mephistopheles, the devil who makes a bargain with Faustus, explains that he is still in hell even if he is on earth talking with Dr. Faustus. This suggests hell is a state of being, regardless of one's physical location.

Although the poet John Milton portrays heaven and hell as spatial sites, he also seems to suggest heaven and hell can be anywhere. "The mind is its own place, and in itself can make a heaven of hell, a hell of heaven" (*Paradise Lost*). I suggest that we think of hell as a state of devastating evil, a ghastly, invidious state where the love of God is spurned or eclipsed; it might involve suffering, but it might also involve a haunting void or vacuum.

PART FOUR: THE EAGLE

The infliction of violent harm on the innocent counts as a case of making the lives of victims hell.

The Gospel of John contains passages that suggest hell can be invoked or created by betrayal or infidelity and contempt of others. I take it that this is at least one of the lessons of the story of the woman accused of adultery (7:53—8:11). (It does not appear in all the old texts of John, but I am convinced it is authentic.) In that story we learn that a betrayal of one's spouse is a sin, but so is the self-righteousness of the persons condemning wrongdoers.

The narrative of the betrayal and trial of Jesus (18:1—19:16) forces us to recognize the horror of betrayal, making false allegations and subjecting an innocent person to torture and death. We are further led to believe that while Sabbath-breaking can be permitted for a great good, enforcing Sabbath rituals can be wrong, especially as the hellish pretext for murdering Jesus.

The positive images of goodness in John can hold up a mirror to show what is hellishly wrong. Being able to recognize the good shepherd helps us to recognize a shepherd who is cruel and brutal. If we see loving God and neighbor as good, we can also see that hating God and neighbor is evil. If sharing food and washing feet are good or heavenly (John 13:1–17), the deprivation of food from starving people and the humiliation of others are hellish.

Creating a hell for others is not hard to imagine: murder, rape, genocide, physical abuse, torture, exploitation, enslavement, harmful manipulation, and more, all make life hellish or hell.

What the Gospels highlight is the hell of wrongdoers who do not repent and renounce their hellish deeds. From the beginning of the Gospel of John, John the Baptist entreats people to recognize and confess their wrongdoing, to repent rather than continue or deepen their abhorrent ways.

In John, forgiveness is important (20:23). Some Christians think that forgiveness of a wrongdoer (hell-maker) does not require the wrongdoer to repent. I can make some sense of this. Imagine that someone who has wronged you died without confessing the wrong and repenting. Perhaps you might forgive by commending the person's soul to God or by renouncing any resentment against that person. There might also be a kind of forgiveness that can be offered in the absence of repentance, as when Anthony Thomson and other Christians in the 2015 Charleston church shooting forgave the shooter, Dylan Roof, who had killed members and had not repented. But without his repentance, *reconciliatory* forgiveness (in which Thompson and others embrace Roof and welcome him into their community) would seem impossible (or at least imprudent and suicidal; he might shoot more of them).

One may love a person who has murdered your companions and even tried to murder you. But embracing, or condoning the murderous acts and intent to do more killing seems to wrongfully align oneself with evil. I am sure Thomson does no such condoning, but the offer of forgiveness without repentance raises a red flag for me because it seems to diminish the importance of repentance before there can be reconciliation. If the murderer is truly unrepentant, there is reason to think he would neither recognize the need for forgiveness nor accept an offer of forgiveness (whether offered by relatives of victims or even God). So, while loving an unrepentant murderer may be Christ-like (and perhaps could be called a type of forgiveness), I think it is vital for Christians to realize the momentous importance of *confession and repentance in the course of seeking human or divine forgiveness and full reconciliation and healing.*

Dominican monk Herbert McCabe, who published some popular books on faith and taught at Oxford, seems to think otherwise. He writes that God's "love for us doesn't depend on what we do or what we are like. He doesn't care whether we are sinners or not. It makes no difference to him." In response, I cannot imagine worshiping a God who doesn't care whether I am a murderer or child-abuser, but perhaps I have taken his words out of context. To guard against such misconstruing, I cite McCabe further:

> [God] is just waiting to welcome us with joy and love. Sin doesn't alter God's attitude towards us; it alters our attitude toward to him, so that we change him from the God who is simply love and nothing else, into the punitive ogre, this Satan. Sin matters enormously to us if

> we are sinners; it doesn't matter at all to God. In a fairly literal sense, he doesn't give a damn about our sins. It is we who give the damns. We damn ourselves because we would rather justify and excuse ourselves and look on our self-serving images of ourselves, than be taken out of ourselves by the infinite love of God. Contrition or forgiveness (remember it is we who forgive ourselves) is almost the exact opposite of excusing ourselves.[49]

In this larger context, McCabe seems to agree that confession and repentance are of enormous importance among humans. But he explains why this is not so, given his view of God:

> God, of course, is not injured or insulted or threatened by our sin. So, when we speak of him forgiving, we are using the word "forgiving" in a rather stretched way, a rather far-fetched way. We speak of God forgiving, not because of anything that happens in God, but because of what happens in us, because of the recreative and redemptive side of forgiveness. All the insult and injury we do in sinning is to ourselves alone, not to God. We speak of God forgiving us because he comes to us to save us from ourselves, to restore us after we have injured ourselves, to redeem and re-create us.[50]

While I relish what McCabe writes about God's redeeming and re-creating, I still suggest that McCabe's God is more aloof and dispassionate than the God revealed in John, the God "who so loved the world that he gave his only begotten Son" to deliver us out of hell. If the Gospel of John is our guide, God's Son was not just injured by human sin, but also savagely tortured and subjected to a humiliating, bloody execution. Even apart from the incarnation, I suggest that it makes perfect sense, theologically, to see all sin as injuring or violating God's will and love of creation. His loving the sinner is not the same as overlooking or being unmoved by the sin.

The beginning of John's Gospel, "In the beginning . . ." echoes the beginning of Genesis, "In the beginning, God created . . . ." If God lovingly created the cosmos as good and for its good then, arguably, our acts to destroy and disfigure that good are violations of the will and nature of God. If this is so, divine forgiveness for such sinful violation is something we do well to seek, as we are encouraged to do in the Lord's Prayer by asking God "to forgive us our trespasses." In some liturgies God is asked to forgive us our debts or sins.

I join Father McCabe in praising a God who is ready to restore, redeem, and save us from the hell we have created and continue to create. But I suggest that for God's saving grace to be effective, we need to confess and to seek God's help in delivering us from the hell we create and impose on others. I suspect that the surest way to be in hell and stay there is by refusing confession and repentance. And for those who suffer hellish torment, but are innocent and thus not in need of confession, repentance, and forgiveness, let us pray that their victimizers repent and that all of us may be delivered from evil—also an element found in the Lord's Prayer.

Chapter 27

Who Needs the Incarnation?

Who needs the incarnation, if one lives a life in light of loving God and one another? Why would one feel any need for a more expansive vision of God and the creation?

Among the four Gospels, John's contains the most explicit testimony of the divinity of Jesus. "In the beginning was the Word, and the Word was with God and the Word was God" (1:1). "Jesus said to them, 'Most assuredly, I say to you, before Abraham was, I Am'" (8:58). "I and the Father are one" (10:30).

Early Christians saw Jesus Christ as wholly God and wholly human. In the words of the fifth-century Council of Chalcedon, Jesus Christ is "at once complete in Godhead and complete in manhood, truly God and truly man" (Acts 5). Understanding the incarnation was tied into the understanding of a triune God, for while Jesus is fully God (*totus Deus*), Jesus is not the whole of God (*totum Dei*). The whole of God is three persons, the Trinity made up of the Father, Son, and Holy Spirit.

More on the Trinity in the next essay. For now, let us consider why the incarnation is so important to Christians, especially in light of the rejection of the incarnation by two of the great historically linked religions, Judaism and Islam. Judaism and Islam both adhere to monotheism; there is one God, not three. Traditionally, Judaism looks forward to the coming of the Messiah, but not the coming of God becoming incarnate. The Qur'an recognizes Jesus' miraculous birth and abilities. Jesus, say Muslims, is the greatest prophet before Mohammed, sent from God as a messianic messenger. Mary, the mother of Jesus, is seen in Islam as the most pure, exalted woman. Both Judaism and Islam see God as just, holy, loving, and merciful. However, neither religion contends that God's loving mercy (or salvation) is dependent upon the sacrifice and resurrection of an incarnate God-man. Historically, Jewish and Muslim philosophers have held that the incarnation is both incoherent, polytheistic, and idolatrous (worshiping a creature rather than the Creator). So, why should Christians give the incarnation special attention?

Some Christians have reinterpreted belief in the incarnation, perhaps in part to reduce the divide between Christianity on the one hand and Judaism and Islam on the other. One strategy is to view the Trinity as three modes or ways in which God is revealed; God is experienced as the creator, redeemer, and sanctifier of the cosmos. This does not commit one to believing that the Godhead contains or consists of three persons. Another is to construe claims about Jesus' divinity as claims that Jesus' will and character was so suffused with God's will and character that Jesus functioned as God among us. On this view, Jesus was not just a messenger. He displayed what one theologian called "God consciousness."

Those, like me, who accept the orthodox creedal teaching of Jesus being fully human and fully God respect these efforts to seek closer accord with Judaism and Islam. Actually, much of my life has been committed to interfaith dialogue. Notwithstanding differences on the incarnation, I have prayed with Jewish and Muslim philosophers, theologians, and clerics on the shared belief that we worship and pray to the same God, even if we disagree on some historical and faith commitments.

Probably my most extraordinary experience of a bond between Christian and Muslim philosophers happened in 2013 when a recent St. Olaf graduate and I, along with two other Christian philosophers, were flown to Iran for a major conference on the Shia philosopher Morteza Motahhari in the holy city of Qom (expenses paid by the Iranians). On arrival we were given flowers, a police escort, interviews on state television, and wonderful philosophical dialogue.

On the second day, I praised Motahhari as not just a martyr, a *shahid*, for his faith and his role in the Iranian revolution, but also for his philosophy. In 1975 he responded with reason and arguments to Marxist critics of the revolution. He was assassinated on May 1, 1979, by the Forqan Group, an anticlerical society. I proposed that the way of philosophy (the love of wisdom) was to always persuade by reason, only resorting to force in self-defense. Motahhari took a risk that led to his death, but his death was a tribute to his commitment to nonviolence and love, not war.

When my words were translated into Farsi, there was an astounding applause; the Ayatollah present stretched out his hand to me. The recent St. Olaf graduate said, "The Ayatollah is giving you a high five!" Maybe, but when the son of Motahhari embraced me, he said the Ayatollah was giving me a blessing.

The point of the story is that we can give each other blessings, even if we disagree about the incarnation. We can learn from each other, as I learned from my Shia Muslim friends when we did a video link between my philosophy class in the United States and a class in Iran, studying Muslim philosopher Avicenna on love.

Love is actually a key element in the historic affirmation of the incarnation. Christian tradition and some others influenced by Plato identify two dimensions of love: beneficent love and unitive love. When you love other people, you desire their good, their benefaction; you also desire to be unified with them. Unitive love in a romantic relationship involves *eros*; while in non-romantic love, you may simply desire to be in the presence of the beloved. From the standpoint of Christianity, the incarnation is the ultimate combination of beneficent and unitive love.

It involves God the Son uniting with human nature, being born of a human mother and living an embodied human life. In his poem "The Divine Image," William Blake delights in the intimate manifestation of God in human form:

> To Mercy, Pity, Peace, and Love
> All pray in their distress;
> And to these virtues of delight
> Return their thankfulness.
>
> For Mercy, Pity, Peace, and Love
> Is God, our father dear,
> And Mercy, Pity, Peace, and Love
> Is Man, his child and care.
>
> For Mercy has a human heart,
> Pity a human face,
> And Love, the human form divine,
> And Peace, the human dress.
>
> Then every man, of every clime,
> That prays in his distress,
> Prays to the human form divine,
> Love, Mercy, Pity, Peace.
>
> And all must love the human form,
> In heathen, Turk, or Jew;
> Where Mercy, Love, and Pity dwell
> There God is dwelling too.[51]

For Blake, the affirmation of the good of the incarnation was tied in with his affirmation and advocacy of the goodness of human life, and his opposition to the exploitation of the poor in his day (child labor and inhumane, life-threatening work conditions).

Actually, in Judaism and Islam, there is something similar to what Christians believe about Jesus as the incarnate Lord. In Judaism, Wisdom is with God in creation (Prov 8:27–30; wisdom is personified in Prov 8:1—9:12). Wisdom is the "pure emanation of the glory of God" (Book of Wisdom 7:25–26, a revered Jewish text, but not part of the Hebrew Bible). To follow Wisdom is to follow God (a theme running throughout the wisdom literature, Proverbs, Ecclesiastes, Job, the Book of Wisdom). Wisdom is not an "in flesh" incarnation, but in Sirach Wisdom comes to dwell in the Torah. Dwelling among us, Wisdom can be seen as an immanent divine presence. For many Muslims the Qur'an that we have on earth was sent by God (17:105); it is the manifestation of the Heavenly Qur'an, which is eternal and uncreated. Again, not an incarnation, but suggestive of the divine being manifested on earth.

This is a book of light essays rather than a work of apologetics. For an excellent work defending the incarnation, see T. V. Morris's *The Logic of God Incarnate*.[52] I end this chapter by noting how Jews, Christians, and Muslims have much to learn from each other.

Avicenna's view of love as the means by which we can find our way home with God can powerfully speak to non-Muslims. The twentieth-century Jewish philosopher Martin Buber, with his stress on personal engagement with God and each other, is a powerful resource to all. Martin Luther King Jr. has much to teach us all about love and nonviolent resistance to injustice. And who doesn't love the poetry of the thirteenth-century Persian Sufi mystic Rumi?

> Love is the
> Water of Life.
> Drink it down
> With Heart and Soul.

One reason that even the possibility of the incarnation excites the imagination and desire of many Christians is the wonder that the God of limitless love, the creator and sustainer of the cosmos, might share in our life, drinking water with us, sharing with heart and soul his body and blood in the form of bread and wine, and showing us in the person of Jesus Christ a concrete, visible manifestation of God's love. Such life-giving power is praised by

Bonaventura in the ecstatic ending of his work *The Tree of Life*, written in the thirteenth century:

> From this Fountain [of life and light]
> flows the stream of the oil of gladness,
> which gladdens the city of God,
> and the powerful fiery torrent,
> the torrent, I say, of pleasure of God
> from which the guests at the heavenly banquet
> drink to joyful inebriation ...
>
> Anoint us
> with this sacred oil
> and refresh
> with its longed-for waters of this torrent
> the thirsting throat of our parched hearts
> so that amid shouts of joy and thanksgiving
> we may sing to you
> a canticle of praise.[53]

Chapter 28

Why the Trinity?

It may sound a bit daft to have favorite parts of different religions, but I do. In Taoism I relish finding the natural way of things. I am attracted to the tradition of filial or family piety or reverence in Confucianism. The fostering of community in Judaism is great. In my view, the Islamic practice of praying five times a day and going on pilgrimage (the Hajj) makes the ordinary lives of Christians look a little too relaxed. In Christianity, among many elements, is the Trinity, God is one in three persons: Father, Son, and Holy Spirit.

Jesus invokes his followers to baptize in the name of the Father, Son, and Holy Spirit in Matthew 28:19-20. While John's Gospel does not refer explicitly to such a trinitarian format, the divinity of the Father and Son seems affirmed (see previous essay) and the role of the Holy Spirit seems to shine through (14:26, 15:26, 16:8-11, 16:13, among many other verses). These scriptural texts led early Christians to understand the Father, Son, and Holy Spirit as distinct (after all, when Jesus prays to the Father, it seems that he is not praying to himself), while still affirming the oneness of God. The theological position I find profoundly important is called *perichoresis* (in Latin, *circumincession*), according to which the three divine persons are united in perfect love and mutual indwelling to form a single essence.[54] Mutual indwelling is suggested in passages like "I am in the Father and the Father is in me" (14:10-11). Augustine would later put this as "Each are in each, and all in each, and each in all, and all are one."[55] Sometimes the unity of persons is described in terms of *coinherence*, a term coined by the Anglican novelist Charles Williams, who was one of the "Inklings," a group that included C. S. Lewis and J. R. R. Tolkien. Williams used *coinherence* to describe how one person can mentally or spiritually enter the life of another to lovingly bear their burdens, relieve their anguish.

Twelfth-century Scottish philosopher Richard of St. Victor articulated this perichoresis theology in terms of God embodying the three highest loves: self-love, love of another, and the love of two for a third.[56] Self-love, as opposed to vanity or narcissism, seems a basic ingredient in any healthy life. Its opposite, self-hatred, is debilitating. However, self-love alone seems insufficient; love of another being seems enriching. Self-love and love of another also seems to naturally lead to love of some further being or thing. Consider a human case and then divine. When they were young, the poets William Wordsworth and Samuel Coleridge each had self-love, they loved each other, and they loved a third thing, the English language. What emerged from their love was the romantic movement in poetry. But when Coleridge started to lose self-love, perhaps from misusing opium, and Wordsworth's self-love was threatened by vanity, their love for each other suffered, as did their poetry.

In the Christian vision of the Godhead, each divine person has self-love, each loves the other, and each pair loves the third. The Father and the Son love the Holy Spirit; the Son and the Holy Spirit love the Father; the Father and the Holy Spirit love the Son. On this view, the Godhead consists of giving and receiving of love; it is the inner glory of God. And it is from the glory of this inner love that God lovingly creates a cosmos.

Because of my devotion to this vision of the Trinity, I have reproductions of Andrei Rublev's icon of the Trinity by my bedside and on my desk. This icon serves as a constant reminder that the triune God calls us into a broader relationship or communion, an anecdote to self-preoccupation and egotism. By one of the icons, I have a card with these lines from the theologian Catherine Mowry LaGuna: "The life of God—precisely because God is triune—does not belong to God alone. God who dwells in inaccessible light and eternal glory comes to us in the face of Christ and the activity of Holy Spirit. Because of God's outreach to the creature, God is said to be essentially relational, ecstatic, fecund, alive as passionate love. Divine life is therefore our life."[57]

The Trinity has its critics. Consider an objection formulated by a friend, a philosophy professor whom I met at a conference on the Trinity in Moscow in 2001. He called it the "Deception Objection." In the Old Testament, God is described as one. "You shall have no other gods before me" (Deut 5:7). Applying the Deception Objection, imagine a girl, Annie, who receives letters and gifts throughout her childhood from a godfather named Frank. She trusts appearances; Frank presents himself as Frank, a single person. But when she comes of age, it is revealed that Frank was not a single person, but three persons who had agreed to represent themselves as a single person. Wouldn't Annie feel shocked and betrayed? My friend argued that the Christian belief that God is triune should also be seen as a shocking betrayal of the biblical injunction that God is one.

Upon hearing this objection, a student in my class got together with ten students. He did a montage photograph of them to form a single face. Using this face and posing as Chris, they gave another unsuspecting student letters and gifts for a week. They then revealed to him that Chris was actually ten people. How did he react? He was amused. He expressed no sense of betrayal.

Back to perichoresis theology. Unlike the story of Annie or the case of my students, the coinherence of Father, Son, and Holy Spirit is believed to be an essential, mutual indwelling. God's manifestation as singular while being tri-personal seems no more shocking than, say, falling in love with a person and later realizing that person's triune nature of body, mind, and spirit.

WHY THE TRINITY?

I suggest that the biblical Old Testament insistence on one God is compatible with the Trinity. In perichoresis theology, God is one in essence, but not homogenous. The fact (if it is one) that the Godhead consists of three persons in perfect union does not deny the singularity of God. One can also point to instances in the Old Testament in which there is some suggestion of a plurality in God. One of the Hebrew terms for God is *Elohim*, a plural noun. In Genesis 1:26 God says, "Let *us* make humans in *our* image . . . ." The narrator then adds, "So God created humans in *his* image" (Gen 1:27). Clearly the one God addresses himself here as "us" and "our." (See also Genesis 11:7 and Isaiah 48:16–17.)

I commend the Christian notion of heaven that suggests we ourselves might come to experience, in small part, something of the richness of a coinherent state of being, not at the level of the essentiality within the Godhead, but with and for each other. The British philosopher A. E. Taylor offers this portrait:

> Heaven, to put it pictorially, is not a realm of selves, each clinging pertinaciously to some secret possession which it will share with no other, but Heaven is a realm of souls for all that, selves whose whole life is one of the supreme adventure, losing themselves in God, but with the result that in the very plunge out of self they find, not nothing, but themselves, and themselves with a richer content.[58]

This is not to say that we might, in heaven, be like Frank in the Annie story or like Chris in the students' performance as Chris. But Taylor points to the possibility that we may someday experience something like a divine giving and receiving of love that reflects the perfection of coinherence in the Godhead.

Chapter 29

Why Care About the Eucharist?

John's Gospel contains the most radical teaching that has informed centuries of Christian liturgy in which bread and wine are consecrated, or blessed, and distributed among the faithful as Christ's body and blood. Jesus says, "Unless you eat the flesh of the Son of Man and drink his blood, you do not have life within you" (6:53). Jesus refers to himself over eighty times as the Son of Man, so he is talking about himself. It is hard to take Jesus' saying literally, as it appears cannibalistic and disgusting. Is Jesus being metaphorical?

I worry about being too quick to turn Christian terms and practices into metaphors. A priest in our church turned almost everything in scripture, liturgy, and creeds into metaphors; his nickname was "the metaphorical Christian." When Jesus distributes bread and wine to his disciples prior to the crucifixion, it is clear that he is not literally distributing his corporeal body and blood. So, we seem to need to affirm that eating and drinking the body and blood of the Lord is something real, but not carnal or merely a metaphor. Moreover, while we might worry about metaphors being overused, metaphorical language can be used truly and with great significance. If you told me that I broke your heart or that your love for me is over the moon, I will be sad or happy appropriately and not complain that you're using metaphors.

While Roman Catholics have defined the transformation of consecrated bread and wine into the body and blood of Jesus, Anglicans and Eastern Orthodoxy have preferred to talk in terms of *the real presence* of Jesus Christ. In the course of the Eucharist, Jesus Christ is said to be sacramentally present. Virtually all Christians affirm the omnipresence of God; there is no place where God is not. God is present in terms of power, knowledge, and accessibility. That is, God creates and sustains the whole of creation. God can act in specific ways, performing miracles anywhere in the cosmos, unconstrained by the laws of nature. God has maximal knowledge of all that is; and God hears and can respond to prayers from anywhere in creation. Being sacramentally present, God signals special moments in space-time where God is encountered through the reading of scripture, prayer, and the re-enacting of the Eucharist. When the words of institution are said, we are invited to eat bread and drink wine together in remembrance that Christ died for us and to feed on him in our hearts with faith and thanksgiving (*Book of Common Prayer*).

One reason to care about the Eucharist is that it is a celebration of the intimacy of the incarnation. Both Gregory of Nyssa and St. Bernard describe the incarnation as a divine kiss. God's uniting with human nature is like a loving kiss. Both Gregory and Bernard develop this language, drawing on the Song of Songs, an erotic romance that many Christians and Jews have treated as an allegory of the love between the soul and God. Drawing on this tradition, some people at a Eucharist service reverently kiss the chalice before drinking the wine. The intimate experience of Christ's sacramental presence can embolden one to see God everywhere.[59]

Consider this joyful sense of God's ubiquity by Clement of Alexandria (first and second centuries). While he defended the Eucharist as a special experience of the presence of Christ, and so not a mere metaphor or symbol, he gave homage to God's omnipresence:

> All our life is a festival: being persuaded that God is everywhere present on all sides, we praise him while we till the ground, we sing hymns when we sail the sea, we feel his inspiration in all we do. [We] enjoy a greater intimacy with God, being at once serious and cheerful on everything, serious owing to our thoughts being turned to heaven, and cheerful as we reckon up the blessings with which God has enriched our human life.[60]

Tolkien himself had a deep devotion to the Eucharist. In 1941, Tolkien wrote about this in a letter to his son Michael:

> Out of the darkness of my life, so much frustrated, I put before you the one great thing to love on earth: the Blessed Sacrament. . . . There you will find romance, glory, honour, fidelity, and the true way of all your loves upon earth, and more than that: Death: by the divine paradox, that which ends life, and demands the surrender of all, and yet by the taste (or foretaste) of which alone can what you seek in your earthly relationships (love, faithfulness, joy) be maintained, or take on that complexion of reality, of eternal endurance, which every man's heart desires.[61]

I suggest that the Eucharist involves what some theologians have called *infused grace*, the infusion or taking in of a divine elixir that can strengthen one's being. This may sound too magical, perhaps aligning the bread and wine of the Eucharist with lembas, the elvish bread in *The Lord of the Rings* that can give one strength for long journeys. I will resort to a more homely, though admittedly bizarre example of how the Eucharist involves inspiration (from the Latin *inspiratus*, meaning "to breathe into").

Dressed in a Santa Claus outfit one Christmas Eve in Georgia, I was driven by car to deliver presents to some children. We were stopped by a police officer. "What seems to be the problem?" I asked. The police officer said that the lit candle I was holding did not generate enough light for safe driving. He said something like,

"Santa, please ask your driver to turn on the car lights." Although mixing theology and safe driving tips may be a stretch, I liken the Eucharist to lighting up our world, enabling us to see or breathe in God's love of us and creation. It broadens our horizon from the comparatively small confine of relying on just ourselves (and, as it were, our individual, sometimes dim candles). By beckoning us to share a meal with others, to be part of a community, the Eucharist can challenge our tendency to think we are self-sufficient individuals. Evelyn Underhill offers us this reminder:

> You remember how Dante says that directly a soul ceases to say *Mine*, and says *Ours*, it makes the transition from the narrow, constricted, individual life to the truly free, truly personal, truly creative spiritual life; in which all are linked together in one single response to the Father of all spirits, God.[62]

Chapter 30

Where Is Heaven?

I suggest that the Gospel of John portrays eternal life as something that is real *now*. In John 17:3, Jesus says, "This is eternal life, that they may know you, the only true God, and Jesus Christ whom you have sent." If such knowledge occurs in this life, eternal life also occurs in this life.

In the often-cited passage John 3:16, those who believe in God and his Son are said "to *have* eternal life." This is not just a future matter, but a current here-and-now state of being. In John 10:10, Jesus says he came so that persons have "life and have it abundantly." In John, chapter 14, Jesus also speaks of preparing a place in life after this life. Theologians have come to see this as an affirmation of realized and future eschatology. The term *eschatology* refers to the study of final things in human and world history. What many theologians see in John is that Jesus' eschatology is not just about what is future.

In eschatology one hears about heaven and hell and sometimes purgatory. If the context is religious diversity or pluralism, then Nirvana, karma, enlightenment, release from the cycle of suffering, ancestral spirits, and more, come into play. For those interested, John Hick, a brilliant philosophical theologian, speculatively constructed a map of a possible afterlife. He draws on multiple traditions in his book *Death and Eternal Life*.

In this essay, let's stick with the Christian view of heaven and address two worries: the problem of space and the problem of time. I then suggest some ways to get to heaven now.

The problem of space. Following the example of Jesus, many Christians believe in the resurrection of the dead. Despite scripture referring to the resurrected body being heavenly or glorified (Phil 3:21; 1 Cor 15), which suggests a different body, many have believed the afterlife bodies will literally be the same body we have when we die (perhaps gloriously transformed). This is why Christians were noted for their special care for the bodies of the dead, and cremation was discouraged. Moreover, some Christians have proposed that the site of resurrected life will be earth.

In the first few centuries of Christianity, earth might have been a plausible location for resurrected life, but with the planet's current population of eight billion, and since our appearance probably another twenty billion to forty billion people, you have a mind-blowing overpopulation issue. The idea that it would be desirable to be resurrected with the same body you had when you died seems to many of us utterly undesirable and perhaps impossible, since many particles of the bodies of the dead have intermingled with other life-forms, including the bodies of other humans. And in some cases, human bodies have been annihilated.

In reply to the problem of space, some Christians have denied the unity of space; they say an omnipotent God can create and sustain indefinitely spatial worlds in multiple universes, not spatially related to this one. Many Christians do not embrace materialism and construe the resurrection as a material re-embodiment of your soul with your body (a body that is newly created as yours, but not numerically identical with your body that was, after death, dis-integrated).

I find it peculiar when a dead body is identified as the person who died rather than as a corpse or remains. After my mother died, I called the funeral home that was overseeing the cremation of her body. The funeral director reported: "We have your mother here." I was tempted to reply: "Great. Put her on the phone!" I was not wanting to be pedantic (I was grieving), but I felt strongly that the funeral home had her *body*, not *her*. While there have been and are Christian materialists, the majority traditional view is that we are more than our material bodies.[63]

In any case, finding spatial realms for life after death is not a problem for an omnipotent God. Perhaps Christians have long had spiritual reasons to posit a multiverse quite independent of contemporary physics and philosophy.

One other vexing spatial issue concerns exclusivity. Dante's *Divine Comedy* pictures hell, purgatory, and heaven or paradise in a kind of hierarchical order. Persons seem to be assigned to various places. Should we picture a multitude of spatial realms in which heaven with Jesus should be the ideal? No less a theologian than Origen of Alexandria entertained such a sequence of stages that souls pass through, and, in our own day, John Hick has proposed something similar. (But as a religious pluralist, Hick sees Christianity as one of many, equally valid paths to salvation or enlightenment.)

I suggest we are not in a position to speculate now about specific locations (presumably, no readers are trying to mail packages to heaven and want to get the address right), but we do well to reject one minority view. From time to time, Christians have held that hell involves everlasting punishment and that one of the joys of those in heaven will be in enjoying such a sight of divine justice. I am in sympathy with the theologian Andrew Hronich when he calls such enjoyment sadistic.[64] Even if universalism (the view that all souls will eventually be saved) is not true, I suggest that all Christians should *hope and pray* that all persons shall be saved. Prayers for all creatures should, I think, be a mark of Christian spirituality.

I agree that some punishments can be curative and good, but not everlasting suffering. The love of all creation should be the goal. The invocation of Father Zosima in Dostoevsky's *Brothers Karamazov* should take primacy over our (sometimes quite understandable) pleasure in punishment. He says:

Love all of God's creation, the whole and every grain of sand in it. Love every leaf, love every ray of God's light. Love the animals, love the plants, love everything. If you will love everything, you will perceive the divine mystery in things. Once you perceive it, you will begin to comprehend it every day. And you will come at last to love the whole world with an all-embracing love.

Love the animals. God has given them the rudiments of thought and joy untroubled. Do not trouble it, don't harass them, don't deprive them of their happiness, don't work against God's intent. Man, do not pride yourself on superiority to the animals; they are without sin, and you, with your greatness, defile the earth with your appearance on it, and leave the traces of your foulness after you—alas, it is true of almost every one of us![65]

The problem of time. Some philosophers have proposed that heaven would be boring. We can imagine that, in the absence of bodily weakness and organ failure, one might take pleasure in being alive over a hundred years, but over five hundred or a thousand years? Arguably, whatever pleasurable activities we imagine, if endlessly repeated they would become vapid and meaningless. Philosopher Stephen Cave has complained that a state of endless bliss would be disastrous:

> A state of permanent bliss for all is one in which we have no individual goals, no traits or quirks to mark us out from one another, no individual personalities at all. It is a state in which we are reduced to less than contented infants, one in which all identity is lost to the extent that is hard to tell apart from oblivion.[66]

On the matter of boredom, I *almost* don't know what to say. This might be a matter of individual personality or imagination. I cannot imagine being bored in some relationships. I find my wife, Jil, fascinating in a way I cannot imagine being exhausted. And in a relationship with God, as described by great Christian mystics, I find a depth of meaning and wonder incapable of erosion.

As for bliss, I don't think heaven has ever been interpreted in scripture, Christian theology, or art and literature as a state of a "permanent bliss" that obliterates our individuality, traits, and quirks, and reduces persons to a sub-infantile state. Rather, it is our individual lives, our virtues and vices, our choices to love or hate, and so on, that can usher in heaven or hell. The experiences I have had that are heavenly often involve joy or happiness, but they certainly have involved individuals who are distinctive and not reduced to ecstatic sub-infants.

Getting to heaven now: There are countless routes to heaven. Heaven may be accessed through loving, healthy friendships; marriage and romance; having and raising children; making art; prayer and meditation—the list is endless. Rather than mention obvious routes, I briefly highlight four markers or signposts that identify those routes: a restive state of being, the reversal of ills, unexpected goods, and play. I am sure there are a hundred others, but these four, in my experience, are worth reporting.

A restive state of being: So often we measure success or even the meaning of our lives in activities. However, I submit there is joy to be found in simply being or, if that sounds too vague, in enjoying the goodness of the moment, such as a meal with family or friends. In Goethe's *Faust*, the main character finally comes to appreciate the goodness of a moment: "Stay, moment, stay, for you are so fair." Enjoying a companionship or a sense of God's presence can be a moment spent in heaven here and now. Evelyn Underhill observes:

> We mostly spend [our] lives conjugating three verbs: to Want, to Have, and to Do. Craving, clutching, and fussing, on the material, political, social, emotional, intellectual—even on the religious plane, we are kept in perpetual unrest: forgetting that none of these verbs have any ultimate significance, except so far as they are transcended by and included in, the fundamental verb, to Be: and that Being, not wanting, having, and doing, is the essence of a spiritual life.[67]

The reversal of ills: I offer just one case. An uncle was visiting me during an election when he realized I was not voting for his candidate. He told me the two most dangerous threats to our nation are terrorists and liberal professors. At one point he said, "Charles, I bet you think I'm full of sh*t."

I said, "If by the phrase 'full of sh*t' I mean I love you and care about what you think and how you feel, that I want to listen to you and have a good exchange. Given that meaning, then, yes, I think you are full of sh*t."

We embraced, temporarily in heaven.

Unexpected goods: My wife, Jil, and I were newcomers at the cathedral. A deacon asked what I was doing. I said that I was considering writing a short story about James Bond. While the films portray Bond as perpetually in his mid-thirties or forties, Ian Fleming, inventor of the fictional character, has him being born in 1924. To honor Bond's turning one hundred in 2024, I was going to portray him coming to church. Later in the week, I received a short story written by the deacon. In the story Bond and one of his villains attended the cathedral, seeking a priest for confession and spiritual direction—probably the only time a person in a religious order wrote a 007 short story to encourage church attendance. We joined the cathedral. Heaven.

Play: G. K. Chesterton contends that heaven is marked by play. I believe that by play he has in mind a joyful interaction involving imagination (or part of the interplay of friendship) that is good in itself, as opposed to work or labor (for example, making a product to be sold in the market). He writes:

> It is not only possible to say a great deal in praise of play; it is really possible to say the highest things in praise of it. It might reasonably be maintained that the true object of all human life is play. Earth is a task garden; heaven is a playground. To be at last in such secure innocence that one can juggle with the universe and the stars, to be so good that one can treat everything as a joke—that may be, perhaps, the real end and final holiday of human souls. When we are really holy we may regard the Universe as a lark.[68]

I think Chesterton has gone a little too far in valorizing the state of treating "everything as a joke." But maybe if there were more playing here on earth, there would be less hell, and heaven itself might just come a little closer.

Chapter 31

Aging Gracefully

The Gospel of John (unlike Matthew and Luke) does not contain an infancy narrative. But it does witness to Jesus coming into the world (1:14) and records Jesus' instruction that we should all be born again: "Truly, I say to you, unless a man is born again, he cannot see the Kingdom of God" (3:3). Jesus says this to a Pharisee, Nicodemus, who asks, "How can a man be born again when he is old?" (3:4). Jesus is not deterred by age, for he replies, "Truly, truly, I say to you, unless one is born of water and the Spirit, he cannot enter the kingdom of God."

In his Gospel, John records the teaching and acts of Jesus over three years, leading up to his crucifixion, death, and resurrection at thirty-three years old (according to early Christian tradition; John does not record Jesus' age). Can we learn anything about aging in John?

For starters, we see that being born and being an infant is good. Not everyone in the ancient world thought so. The greatest philosopher in late antiquity, Plotinus, thought of birth as an ill, because it was then that one's soul acquired a body, which was an encumbrance. In fact, today some people called anti-natalists think that there are good reasons not to reproduce and bring children up in our dangerous world. On the other hand, Jesus seems to so greatly value birth, he insists that all should seek to be born a second time.

Second, the Gospel of John suggests that aging and ongoing life are good, otherwise there would be no reason for Jesus to raise Lazarus from the dead (chapter 11). As in the case of infancy, not everyone saw aging as a good. Aristotle valued life when one is able-bodied and strong in thought and action, but he lamented aging when we weaken and lose our vigor. Jesus' practice of healing (curing a person who was ill for thirty-eight years, restoring sight to the blind, chapters 5 and 9) reveals his valuing health, to be sure, but his teaching about being born again suggests that such rebirth can occur at any stage in life. Jesus is not put off by Nicodemus's worry about how someone old may be reborn.

In the second century, St. Irenaeus confirms the above points about the good of birth, infancy, and aging:

> He came to save all through Himself—all, I say, who through Him are reborn in God—infants and children, and youths and old men. Therefore He passed through every age, becoming an infant for infants, sanctifying infants; a child for children, sanctifying those who are of that age, and at the same time becoming for them an example of piety, of righteousness, and submission; a young man for youths, becoming an example for youths and sanctifying them for the Lord. So He became an old man for old men so that He may be the perfect teacher in all things—perfect not only in respect to the setting forth of truth, but perfect in respect to relative age—sanctifying the elderly, and at the same time becoming an example to them. Then He even experienced death itself, so that He might be the firstborn from the dead, having the first place in all things, the originator of life, before all and preceding all.[69]

While I think St. Irenaeus is right on, I suspect that Jesus' teaching suggests that youthfulness is a special value. By youthfulness, I do not mean being young in age, but having energy, being open to Jesus' new commandment: "A new commandment

I give to you, that you love one another, even as I have loved you" (John 13:34). Jesus does not give this commandment in a way that is age-specific. It seems to apply whether we are young or old in age. In predicting Peter's death in old age (John 21:18), Jesus persists in the call he made to Peter when Peter was young: "Follow me!" (21:19). To follow Jesus when one is old in age seems to require renewed youthful energy.

If the above suggestion is right, it may be one reason for being in awe of older persons of faith. One might revere them as parents, grandparents, teachers, benefactors, or repositories of wisdom. But one may also revere the elderly because they have been youthful longer than we who are younger in age.

Chapter 32
Jesus and the Problem of Evil

A curator of a California museum told me of an occasion when his museum hosted thirty children and gave them pencils and paper. One girl was drawing with furious energy. A teacher asked her what she was drawing. The girl replied that she was drawing God. The teacher said, "But, darling, no one knows what God looks like." The girl replied, "They will in about two minutes."

If John's Gospel is right, we do have access to what God looks like. The Gospel proclaims: "No one has seen God at any time, the only begotten God, who is in the bosom of the Father, he has made him known" (1:18). In John's Gospel we further read that if you see Jesus, you have seen the Father (14:8–10). This is why in Renaissance art a holy book is sometimes represented with the Latin inscription *Qui me videt videt et Patrem* (He who sees me sees the Father). Other common inscriptions on books in paintings feature other passages from John: *Ego sum via, veritas, et vita* (I am the way, the truth, and the life), *Ego sum lux mundi* (I am the light of the world), and *Ego sum resurrectio* (I am the resurrection).

John depicts a cosmos in which there is real evil: there is darkness, Satan (the father of lies), desecration (treating the temple sacrilegiously), imprisonment of the innocent (John the Baptist and Jesus), betrayal and violence, including torture and execution. But for all that, there is a steady flow of testimony that in addressing evil, we need to look to the one who proclaimed "I am the resurrection" (as depicted in some paintings of book covers, *Ego Sum resurrectio*).

It seems that John never offers a depiction of evil without giving us a glimpse of the reality of the way to overcome evil by the power of God through Jesus. From ancient times till today, some people have attempted to deny the reality of evil. Evolutionary biologist Richard Dawkins claims:

> The universe that we observe has precisely the properties we should expect if there is, at bottom, no design, no purpose, no evil, no good, nothing but pitiless indifference.[70]

Alternatively, some philosophers think there is so much evil in the cosmos, there cannot be an all-good God. Christians traditionally part company with both the deniers of evil and with those who think the amount of evil should lead us to atheism or, worse, lead us to believe that life is not worth living. G. K. Chesterton considers the dire but absurd consequences if humans were to sincerely believe life is not worth living. He writes:

> At any innocent tea-table we may easily hear a man say, "Life is not worth living." We regard it as we regard the statement that it is a fine day; nobody thinks it can have any serious effects on the man or the world. And yet if that utterance were really believed, the world would stand on its head. Murderers would be given medals for saving men from life; firemen would be denounced from keeping men from death; poisons would be used as medicines; doctors would be called in when people were well; the Royal Humane Society would be rooted out like a horde of assassins.[71]

I am inclined to agree with Chesterton. We find it hard to adopt the view that life is not worth living, and it is just as hard to think of evil (and good) as illusory.

I co-edited a six-volume book series called *The History of Evil*. In my experience of good and evil and in decades teaching, speaking, and writing about evil, I have found matters often come down to these two questions: *Si Deus est, unde malum? Si non est, unde bonum?* (If God exists, why is there evil? If there is no God, why is there good?). Evelyn Underhill may have had these questions in mind when she conceded that Christian spirituality may not explain evil and suffering, but then she went on to claim what Christian spirituality can do:

> [It] does show us how to deal with [evil and suffering]. It insists that something has gone wrong, and badly wrong, with the world. That world as we know it does not look like the work of a loving Father whom the Gospels call us to worship; but rather, like the work of selfish and undisciplined children who have been given wonderful material, and not used that freedom well. Yet we see in this muddled world a constant struggle for Truth, Goodness, Perfection; and all those who give themselves to that struggle—the struggle for the redemption of the world from greed, cruelty, injustice, selfish desire and their results—find themselves supported and reinforced by a spiritual power, which enhances life, strengthens will, and purifies character. And they come to recognize more and more in that power the action of God. These facts are as real as the other facts, which distress and puzzle us; the apparent cruelty, injustice, and the futility of life. We have to account somehow for the existence of gentleness, purity, self-sacrifice, holiness, love; and how can we account for them, unless they are attributes of Reality?[72]

As an aside in this closing chapter, I note that in the above passage Underhill references "the Gospels," hence all four of the Gospels used in this tetramorphic collection of essays.

Back to the problem of evil: lots of arguments have been lined up concerning both questions about why there is evil and good; and I provide some suggested leads to answers in the reference section of this book.[73]

Speaking personally, I am solidly of the mind that there is evil and, in an odd sense, it is good that evil is a problem. If we treat evil as illusory or view it as a natural occurrence, we begin to accommodate it, rather than resist and fight evil. If John and the other Gospels and virtually all Christian tradition is right, evil is abhorrent to God. And Jesus, the prophets, and the saints have been sent to show us the way to be delivered from evil.

One beautiful passage about following Jesus comes at the ending of W. H. Auden's *For the Time Being: A Christmas Oratorio*. It is based on John 14:6: "Jesus answered, 'I am the way, the truth, and the life.'" Auden's poem was written in a time of great suffering, 1942, when it was not at all obvious that the Allies would be victorious over Imperial Japan and Nazi Germany. Here is the end of Auden's oratorio:

> He is the Way.
> Follow Him through the land of Unlikeness;
> You will see rare beasts, and have unique adventures.
>
> He is the Truth.
> Seek Him in the Kingdom of Anxiety;
> You will come to a great city that has expected your return for years.
>
> He is the Life.
> Love Him in the World of the Flesh;
> And at your marriage all its occasions shall dance for joy.[74]

Perhaps in following this way, truth, and life we might find joy even in desperate, evil times. Tolkien portrays such in his classic *The Lord of the Rings*. During a time of great peril, when all reasons for hope seem dashed, and death and defeat appear to be immanent, one of the characters, Pippin, hears Gandalf, the wizard, laugh. Not a cruel or nervous laugh, but something life-affirming, even against all odds.

Pippin glanced in some wonder at the face close beside his own, for the sound of that laugh had been gay and merry. Yet in the wizard's face he saw at first only lines of care and sorrow: though as he looked more intently he perceived that under all there was a great joy: a fountain of mirth enough to set a kingdom laughing, were it to gush forth.[75]

Endnotes

1. My review "Bad for You" was published in *TLS / Times Literary Supplement*, Feb. 12, 1993, 23.

2. Herodotus narrates the Battle of Thermopylae in his *Histories*, book 3: www.livius.org/sources/content/herodotus/herodotus-on-thermopylae/.

3. See Charles Taylor, *A Secular Age* (Cambridge, MA: Harvard University Press, 2007), 681.

4. Professor Paul Reasoner and I facilitated "A Prison Philosopher: A Personal Essay," by Alexander Brown (https://www.mdpi.com/2077-1444/14/4/492#:~:text).

5. Margaret Taliaferro, *In the Beginning: An Account of the Old Testament for Young People* (West Conshohocken, PA: Infinity, 2003).

6. Frodo's laughter occurs in the chapter "The Stairs of Cirith Ungol," in J. R. R. Tolkien, *The Two Towers* (London: George Allen & Unwin, 1954).

7. I recommend Joachim Jeremias, *The Parables of Jesus* (London: SCM, 2003).

8. Charles Taliaferro, *A Narnian Vision of the Atonement: A Defense of the Ransom Theory* (Eugene, OR: Cascade, 2022).

9. See also Charles Taliaferro, "A Shakespearean Account of Redemption," in *The Psychology of Character and Virtue*, edited by Craig Steven Titus (Washington, DC: The Catholic University of America Press, 2009), 42–55.

I recommend Piero Boitani, *The Gospel According to Shakespeare*, translated by V. Montemaggi and R. Jacoff (Notre Dame, IN: University of Notre Dame Press, 2013).

10. For an important resource, see P. Zaleski and C. Zaleski, *Prayer: A History* (Boston: Houghton Mifflin, 2005).

ENDNOTES

On the Jesus prayer and how repetition can be fruitful or sterile, see Timothy Ware, *The Art of Prayer* (London: Faber and Faber, 1966).

11. Vaclav Havel, *Letters to Olga* (New York: Knopf, 1988), 331–32.

12. Thomas Erskine, cited by C. S. Lewis in *Miracles* (San Francisco: HarperCollins, 2000), 129.

13. Oliver Sacks, *Letters*, edited by Kate Edgar (New York: Knopf, 2024), 127.

14. W. H. Auden, "Funeral Blues," https://allpoetry.com/funeral-blues.

15. G. K. Chesterton, *Orthodoxy* (London: 1908), www.ccel.org/ccel/c/chesterton/orthodoxy/cache/orthodoxy.pdf or http://www.ccel.org/ccel/chesterton/orthodoxy.html.

16. See C. S. Lewis, *The Chronicles of Narnia* (San Francisco: HarperCollins, 2001), 72.

17. See J. R. R. Tolkien, *The Return of the King* (London: George Allen & Unwin, 1954).

18. I am indebted to J. Andrew Doole, "Observational Comedy in Luke 15," *Neotestamentica* 50.1 (2016) 181–210.

19. Michel de Montaigne, "On the Education of Children" (1580), https://hyperessays.net/pdf/essays/on-the-education-of-children-A4.pdf. For a positive case for the role of pleasure in education, see Stewart Goetz, *C. S. Lewis on Higher Education: The Pedagogy of Pleasure* (London: Bloomsbury, 2023).

20. See C. S. Lewis, *Miracles* (San Francisco: HarperOne, 2015), chapter 16.

21. Find W. H. Auden's quotation at https://quotefancy.com/quote/984441/.

22. See Charles Taylor, *Sources of the Self: The Making of the Modern Identity* (Cambridge, MA: Harvard University Press, 1989), 50.

23. In *The Golden Cord: A Short Book on the Secular and the Sacred* (Notre Dame, IN: University of Notre Dame Press, 2012), I address God's relationship with time.

24. For a look at how Christianity transformed relations of males and females from Roman imperial times, see Rodney Stark, *The Rise of Christianity: A Sociologist Reconsiders History* (Princeton, NJ: Princeton University Press, 1996).

25. See Colin Morris, *The Discovery of the Individual, 1050–1200* (Toronto: University of Toronto Press, 1987).

26. Find the quotation by Aelred of Rievaulx in his book *Spiritual Friendship*, translated by Mary Laker (Kalamazoo, MI: Cistercian, 1974), 56.

27. See William Langland, *Piers the Ploughman*, translated by J. F. Goodridge (Harmondsworth, UK: Penguin, 1966), 220–21.

28. Tom Wright, *Justification: God's Plan and Paul's Vision* (London: SPCK, 2009).

29. Tertullian, *Apology*, in *The Faith of the Early Fathers*, edited by William Jurgens (Collegeville, MN: Liturgical, 1979), 116.

30. St. Ambrose is cited by Aelred of Rievaulx in *Spiritual Friendship*, translated by Mary Laker (Kalamazoo, MI: Cistercian, 1974), 108.

On food and philosophy, see Michel Le Gall and Charles Taliaferro, "Friendship, Food, Freedom, Fun, and the Future," in *Anthony Bourdain and Philosophy*, edited by Scott Calef (Chicago: Open Universe, 2023), 53–64.

31. Read more about Evelyn Underhill in Margaret Cropper, *The Life of Evelyn Underhill*, (Woodstock, VT: Skylight Paths, 2003), 56.

32. The quotation on reading "a bloodthirsty newspaper at breakfast" comes from a book based on four broadcast talks given in 1936: Evelyn Underhill, *The Spiritual Life* (Eastford, CT: Martino Fine Books, 2013), 135.

33. G. K. Chesterton, *Charles Dickens: A Critical Study* (1906), https://www.gutenberg.org/ebooks/68682.

34. From *Book of Common Prayer*, a prayer for travelers: "O God, our heavenly Father, whose glory fills the whole creation, and whose presence we find wherever we go: Preserve those who travel, in particular (name); surround them with your loving care; protect them from every danger; and bring them in safety to their journey's end; through Jesus Christ our Lord. Amen."

35. See Charles Taliaferro, *Love, Love, Love and Other Essays: Light Reflections on Love, Life, and Death* (Lanham, MD: Rowman and Littlefield, 2006).

36. See Luis de León, *Luis de León: The Names of Christ* (1583), translated by Manuel Durán and William Kluback (New York: Paulist, 1984).

37. On animals and Christianity: Andrew Linzey, *Animal Rites: Liturgies of Animal Care* (London, UK: SCM, 1999).

38. See *Sources of the Self*, by Charles Taylor (Cambridge, MA: Harvard University Press, 1989), 50.

39. Find an account of the martyrdom of St. Polycarp in *The Faith of the Early Fathers*, edited by William A. Jurgens (Collegeville, MN: Liturgical, 1970), 31.

40. See "*Hortus conclusus*" in Lucia Impelluso, *Nature and Its Symbols*, translated by Stephen Sartarelli (Los Angeles: J. Paul Getty Museum, 2004), 12–15.

41. St. Ignatius of Antioch, "Letter to the Philadelphians," in *The Faith of the Early Fathers*, edited by William A. Jurgens (Collegeville, MN: Liturgical, 1970), 22.

42. See Charles Taliaferro, "Prayer," in *The Routledge Companion to Philosophy of Religion*, edited by Chad Meister and Paul Copan (London: Routledge,

2008), 183–200.

43. Peter Kreeft wrote seven dialogues in which Socrates questions philosophers after they have died. See, for example, *Socrates Meets Hume: The Father of Philosophy Meets the Father of Modern Skepticism* (San Francisco: Ignatius, 2010).

44. See G. K. Chesterton, *St. Francis of Assisi* (1923), http://www.gkc.org.uk/gkc/books/.

45. See Charles Taliaferro, "Religious Rites," in *The Cambridge Companion to Christian Philosophical Theology*, edited by Charles Taliaferro and Chad Meister (Cambridge: Cambridge University Press, 2009), 189–200.

46. I was defending a central argument in my book *Consciousness and the Mind of God* (Cambridge: Cambridge University Press, 1994). My critic came around when he read a later defense of my position.

47. See the preface to Evelyn Underhill's *Practical Mysticism: A Little Book for Normal People* (1914. Reprint, New York: Vintage, 2003), https://www.gutenberg.org/ebooks/21774.

48. Two engaging recent works defend Christian universalism:

Andrew Hronich, *Once Loved Always Loved: The Logic of Apokatastasis* (Eugene, OR: Wipf & Stock, 2023). Alvin Kimel, *Destined for Joy: The Gospel of Universal Salvation* (No loc: The Works of George MacDonald, 2022).

For an important overview of the arguments, see *Universal Salvation? The Current Debate*, edited by Robin A. Parry and Christopher Partridge (Carlisle, UK: Paternoster, 2003).

49. Herbert McCabe, "Forgiveness," in *Faith Within Reason*, edited by Brian Davies (London: Continuum Icons, 2007), 157.

50. Herbert McCabe, *God, Christ and Us* (London: Continuum Icons, 2005), 122.

51. William Blake, "The Divine Image" (1789), https://www.poetryfoundation.org/poems/43656/the-divine-image.

52. See Thomas V. Morris, *The Logic of God Incarnate* (Reprint, Eugene, OR: Wipf & Stock, 2001).

53. Bonaventure, *The Soul's Journey into God, The Tree of Life, The Life of St. Francis*, translated by E. Cousins, Classics of Western Spirituality (New York: Paulist, 1978), 171.

54. See Stephen Davis's "Perichoretic Monotheism: A Defense of a Social Theory of the Trinity," in *The Trinity: East/West Dialogue*, edited by M. Y. Stewart (Boston, MA: Kluwer, 2003), 35–52.

55. See St. Augustine, *On the Trinity*, book 6, chapter 10, https://www.

logoslibrary.org/augustine/trinity/0610.html#:~:text.

56. Richard of St. Victor, "[Book III of] *On the Trinity,*" in *Richard of St. Victor,* translated by G. Zinn (New York: Paulist, 1979), 371–97.

57. Catherine Mowry LaGuna, *God for Us: The Trinity and Christian Life* (San Francisco: HarperCollins, 1991), 1.

58. A. E. Taylor, *The Faith of a Moralist* (London: Macmillan, 1951), 308.

59. See Charles Taliaferro, "Religious Rites," in *The Cambridge Companion to Christian Philosophical Theology,* edited by Charles Taliaferro and Chad Meister (Cambridge: Cambridge University Press, 2009), 189–200.

60. Clement of Alexandria, *Stromateis* VII.iii.16, in *Alexandrian Christianity,* edited by Henry Chadwick and J. E. L. Oulton, Library of Christian Classics (Louisville, KY: Westminster John Knox, 1954), vol. 2, 102.

61. *The Letters of J. R. R. Tolkien,* edited by Humphry Carpenter, with Christopher Tolkien (London: George Allen & Unwin, 1981), 53–54.

62. Evelyn Underhill, *The Spiritual Life* (Eastford, CT: Marino Fine Books, 2013), 29–30.

63. On Christianity and the body-soul relationship, see *St. Andrews Encyclopaedia of Theology,* https://www.saet.ac.uk/Christianity/Mindand Consciousness.

See also the entry "Afterlife" in the free online *Stanford Encyclopedia of Philosophy,* https://plato.stanford.edu/entries/afterlife/.

64. See Andrew Hronich, *Once Loved Always Loved: The Logic of Apokatastasis* (Eugene, OR: Wipf & Stock, 2023).

65. Fyodor Dostoevsky, *The Brothers Karamazov,* translated by Richard Pevear and Larissa Volokhonsky (New York: Vintage Classics, 1991), 319.

66. On the problem of bliss: Stephen Cave and John Martin Fischer, *Should You Choose to Live Forever? A Debate* (London: Routledge, 2024), 25.

67. Evelyn Underhill, *The Spiritual Life* (Eastford, CT: Marino Fine Books, 2013), 24–25.

68. G. K. Chesterton, *All Things Considered,* in the complete works of Chesterton, at http://www.gkc.org.uk/gkc/books/.

69. St. Irenaeus, "Against Heresies," in *The Faith of the Early Fathers,* translated by William A. Jurgens (Collegeville, MN: Liturgical, 1970), 31.

70. Richard Dawkins, *River Out of Eden: A Darwinian View of Life* (New York: Basic, 1996).

71. G. K. Chesterton, *Heretics* (1905) (New York: Barnes and Noble, 2007), 2–3.

ENDNOTES

72. Evelyn Underhill, *The Spiritual Life* (Eastford, CT: Marino Fine Books, 2013), 124–25.

73. Charles Taliaferro, *Cascade Companion to Evil* (Eugene, OR: Cascade, 2020). I also address the problem of evil in *The Golden Cord: A Short Book on the Secular and the Sacred* (Notre Dame, IN: University of Notre Dame Press, 2012). Consult also *The History of Evil*, edited by Chad Meister and Charles Taliaferro, 6 vols. (London: Routledge, 1996).

74. Evelyn Underhill, *The Spiritual Life* (Eastford, CT: Marino Fine Books, 2013), 124–25.

75. J. R. R. Tolkien, *The Return of the King* (Boston: Houghton Mifflin, 1994), 31.

www.ingramcontent.com/pod-product-compliance
Lightning Source LLC
Chambersburg PA
CBHW022120160426
43197CB00009B/1100